Endorsements

When Marcia Fisher led me in a prayer of repentance for occultism, something caused me to laugh in disbelief about the generational sin I was repenting from. I realized I was not laughing, but a spirit was making me laugh without my control; she called it a mocking spirit. As a Christian for almost 13 years, this was the first time I had experienced firsthand that a spirit could oppress a Christian. When Marcia prayed for that spirit to leave, I was healed of the recurring vocal chord nodules that plagued me almost 13 years. I was finally able to audition and join my church music team. Later after completing the For My Life™ program at Pleasant Valley Church, I was set free of a lifetime of sleep and depression medications. Also I have had no recurrence of the breast cancer from which God healed me.

Earlier that week at the seminar Marcia taught on the dangers of occultism, and she understands the connection between the occult and health problems. In her quest for healing, she became an astrologer and sought an Indian guru – only to end up so debilitated with Multiple Chemical Sensitivities that she could not leave her home without wearing a mask. It was her experience of repenting from these new age practices and her subsequent miraculous healing that led me to use her as an authority and witness to the hazards of the occult for the TBN Healing Special, "A Night of Miracles." If you think involvement with the occult is harmless, or it may hurt others but could not hurt you, I suggest you read Marcia's book and think again.

Michelle Morey, Associate Producer – "A Night of Miracles" – Trinity Broadcasting Network

D1133337

When I first heard Marcia teach on occultism at Pleasant Valley Church, I sat on the edge of my seat. It was a subject I knew very little about, but Marcia changed this. Many people, both inside and outside the church, will be shown the insidiousness of occultism, and the effect it has on their lives through reading her testimony. I am indebted to Marcia as she has enabled me to minister to others who have occultism in their lives. Many people will be freed as a result of reading this book. Praise God.

> **Therefore my people are gone into captivity, because they have no knowledge: and their honourable men are famished, and their multitude dried up with thirst. Isaiah 5:13**

Teresa Burgess, Co-director of Be In Health, U.K.

In the Bible, God is very clear. He says that we are not to harden our hearts as in rebellion. Marcia Fisher did not know that she was in rebellion against God, but she was not living in obedience to His Son, Jesus Christ. As a result of this, all kinds of sickness became part of her life, sicknesses that today many people suffer from but do not know how to be set free. They have participated with Satan, and he has enslaved them. The Holy Spirit convicted her, and when she reached "the end of her rope," Jesus placed a ministry there, Pleasant Valley Church, that not only brought her healing and deliverance from Satan and all the powers of his deception, but most important of all, brought salvation. Jesus Christ has now become a part of life, and it is her hope that He, and her testimony of His grace, will set others free. She tells how Satan deceived her and how she came to salvation and healing. It is a must read by every born-again believer today, and by every non-believer who wants to know the truth.

Lindley H. Jacobson, Pastor, Silas Ministry

I just finished reading *A New Song for Marcia* which is about a woman who did everything she wanted to do in another life and then discovered that Satan was leading her into a sickness unto death. Her recovery through ministry and prayer by Pastor Henry Wright and his staff is a great testimony. I recommend this book for all Christian bookshelves.

Rev. Dr. Stan Patterson, Retired Methodist Pastor

Marcia Fisher has woven an incredible retelling of her journey from darkness into God's sustaining light. Her transformation is a miracle from God.

Anita Hill, Associate Pastor at Pleasant Valley Church, Thomaston GA; Vice President of Be in Health™ Global; author of *Out of Many Waters*

A New Song For Marcia

By

Marcia Sue Fisher

A True Story of Healing and Transformation

A NEW SONG FOR MARCIA

By Marcia Sue Fisher

Published by Be in Health ™

4178 Crest Highway
Thomaston, GA 30286
www.beinhealth.com
800-453-5775

Front cover design by Zendra Manley
Front cover photograph by Anita Hill
Interior photo editing by Scott Iwahashi
Back cover design by Zendra Manley
Back cover photograph by Zendra Manley

Library of Congress Control Number: 2007908864
Autobiography, Christianity, Healing, Occultism
International Standard Book Number: 978-1-L 60530-258-4

Printed in the United States of America

DEDICATION

In loving memory of my parents

George and Faye Fisher

Acknowledgements

I want to thank Father God, Jesus and the Holy Spirit for my salvation, my deliverance, and my healing. I am very grateful to Pastors Henry W. and Donna Wright of Pleasant Valley Church for their ministry of healing and deliverance and for their obedience to God to follow His calling. Thank you, Pastor Henry, for all that you have done to help restore the lives of people suffering with MCS/EI. I thank Nellie Lower for her love and her discipleship via the telephone, Sharon Dawson for her ministry and love, and Pastor Anita Hill for being a friend in this journey.

I wish to express appreciation to my friends who helped me edit this manuscript: Janet Epperson, Lori Colley, Bruce and Roseanne Gridley, Anita Hill, Pat Koralewski, Karen Kelly, Kate Marston, Beverly McLaughlin, Stan and Nancy Patterson.

I give special thanks to Zendra Manley for designing the book cover.

I thank those who helped me with their expertise in computers: Nancy Patterson, Johnnie Ann Gaskell, and Scott Iwahashi.

I will always appreciate my mother because she did not abandon me, as happens to many with MCS/EI, and she never lost faith in my ability to get well. I dedicate this book to her memory.

x

TABLE OF CONTENTS

Endorsements i

Acknowledgements ix

Forward xiii

Introduction xvi

Daddy's Little Girl.. 1

School Days... 15

Living in Italy 23

Communist Experience... 29

First Love 35

Becoming a Hippy... 41

From Europe to Afghanistan... 49

Following the Guru 63

More Occultism 75

Environmental Illness 87

Disability 99

Meeting the LORD 109

The Miracle Begins... 123

Taking Back My Life 133

Healing through Ministry 143

Returning Home 155

More Walk-out 163

Appendix A (Scripture)... 177

Appendix B (Doctor's Letter)... 185

Appendix C (Victory List) 187

Forward

Marcia was saved through our ministry, and her salvation is truly a miracle. If they were writing the Bible today, she would get at least a chapter, if not a book devoted to the story of her salvation.

I remember when she came to me after she was saved, and God was healing her, and she wanted to talk with me about astrology. She was filled with the Holy Ghost, but she would not fall out of agreement with astrology. She had been trying to help people by identifying with the sun, moon, and stars and the 14th quadrant of the 7th cusp of whatever. It sounded like a cornfield somewhere to me, but she firmly believed that the whole system of astrology identified the present and the future for us. And to know that future would give us great wisdom, and there would be God in it. That is exactly what horoscopes and astrology attempt to do is give you information about the future, whether you are going to have a good day or a bad day. Do you realize how many people consult with mediums and astrologers? Do you know how many Christians consult on this level? Lots of them.

Marcia had developed a position and she was ready to debate it with me. She made an appointment to come to my office, and she was intending to prove to me that I was wrong about my position on astrology and to make me a disciple of astrology. I sat for about an hour listening to her, and I did not say anything. When she was finished she sat back with this look of - "I have convinced you." I did not doubt that she had a desire to help people. I did not doubt the integrity of her motives, because she had a sincere heart. Many people are sincere, but they are sincerely wrong. Ignorance is a form of knowledge. In Isaiah 5:13 God said, "Therefore my people have gone into captivity because they have no knowledge."

Well, I listened to Marcia and I said, "That is very interesting, and I don't doubt the fact that you really want to help people, but I have some difficulty in something." She asked, "What is that?" I said, "When you go to astrology you are looking and identifying according to your precepts and your modalities of thinking what is, and that what it represents is who you are in creation, in the sun, moon and stars, and that is going to be your day. And that is who you are, whether you have the characteristics of a Leo, or a Libra, or a Sagittarius or whatever. That is who you are. And everything that is going to happen to you in the future rotates around this predetermined aspect of your nature and existence. In fact if you continue with this type of thinking you are binding people to what is. And I can't go with it."

"My Bible says nothing is impossible with God. All things are possible to them that believe, and from glory to glory we are being changed into His image. In astrology there is no changing into His image, if you have a defect in your nature, you are stuck with it. If you are going to have a bad day, you had better be prepared for it, because it is coming and there is nothing you can do about it. If you are going to have a blessed day there is nothing you can do about it either. It is in the stars and you are binding people to what is, and you are in fact preaching a gospel of fatalistic thinking, fatalism." And she looked at me and the light went on. She said, "I can't do that; I can't bind people to what is. You are right Pastor, astrology binds people to what they are and what will happen tomorrow. Look at what God has done for me already. And I was stuck in all that occultism; now I am changed." And instantly years and years of a mindset disappeared, didn't disappear, but became inferior to a superior way of thinking. Isn't that what the mind of Christ is?

This book is the story of Marcia's life, her successes and her failures, her sin issues and her subsequent disabling illness. It is about her salvation, deliverance and healing. I recommend this book to Christians and non-Christians alike. If God would do it for her, He would do it for others.

Pastor Henry W. Wright

Sr. Pastor, Pleasant Valley Church, Inc.

Introduction

Pastor Henry W. Wright has taught about spiritual roots to disease in his book, *A More Excellent Way™*. Spiritual roots are those sin issues in our life that cause us to be ill in the first place. However, not all disease is spiritually rooted; Pastor Wright says that approximately eighty percent of disease has its foundation in sin issues. Without being graphic, I have been transparent to expose those sin issues in my life and in the lives of my ancestors.

I was fifty years old when I first asked Jesus into my heart, so I had done a lot of living before then without knowing God. It is not my intention to glorify Satan; however, I must talk about the sin in my life to give you an appreciation for what God has done. I want you to know without a doubt that God loves the sinner!

I always thought I was a free spirit who was in the forefront of any movement or trend in society. I had taken pride in the fact that I was *avant-garde*, or so I thought. Actually, I was a pawn of the Devil taken captive at his will. I was very much a child of the 70's and into sex, drugs, and rock and roll. Then I followed a classic guru experience that led me deep into the occult. The experience in the occult paralleled my descent into illness and disability.

All the while the enemy was enticing me, God had his hand on my life. He knew the end from the beginning. He protected me from going to jail, from diseases unto death, and from ending my own life. I wanted to die but believed that was not acceptable in God's eyes. The Lord drew me to Himself against all odds. It is not a bad thing to become desperate. I needed that in order to be open to Him.

I want to begin with the lives of my parents and grandparents to show you how inherited iniquities and gifts affected my life. Many of you will discern the open doors in the lives of my parents and myself through which the enemy got a foothold. As an adult, I take responsibility for the choices I made, but I paid a dear price for those choices.

I have used some fictitious names in this story, as I am not in contact with some old friends and do not have their permission to use their names. The opinions expressed here are my own, and I have given credit to those who were my teachers. None of what I say is to be construed as medical advice; I am merely telling the story of my descent into illness and the subsequent deliverance and healing I received after I accepted Jesus into my heart. Let's get started!

I waited patiently for the LORD; and he inclined unto me, and heard my cry. He brought me up also out of an horrible pit, out of the miry clay, and set my feet upon a rock, and established my goings. And he hath put a new song in my mouth, even praise unto my God: many shall see it, and fear, and shall trust in the LORD. Psalms 40:1-3

The Fisher family
1942

Chapter One

Daddy's Little Girl

I woke up in the morning and immediately went to my radionics machine to dial away my symptoms. I had put a Polaroid picture of myself in a compartment or well within the machine, so that the machine could identify whom it was treating with healing energy. Then I set the dials to the correct readings for the symptom from which I was suffering. Every disease and every symptom had its own energy reading. There was a black plate attached to the radionics machine that was slippery. I would rub my fingers on the plate until I would get a "stick" or a resistance. This would give me a correct reading for the dials. Then, I would flip the switch and send healing vibrations to myself or into the homeopathic remedy I was concocting. I wrote out an affirmation and put it in the well so these words of healing would also be transported to my spirit.

How did a nice, quiet girl like me, coming from a relatively normal family, having graduated from the University of California with a master's degree, come to rely on such an absurd healing modality as radionics? Scientifically speaking, the radionics machine did not put out enough energy to turn on a light bulb. How could it kill parasites, viruses, candida and heal Environmental Illness? Yet people put their faith in such devices to heal AIDS or even cancer. Radionics is illegal in this country for any use outside of agriculture. That, somehow, made it more enticing. How did I come to rely upon, even prefer, alternative medical practices based on invisible energies? What were the conditions

1

that made me ripe for disabling illness? Let me tell you how I began a descent into spiritual blindness, mental confusion and nearly complete physical breakdown. This is the old song, before God put a new song into my heart. I will start with my family background; however, this is the old song.

My father was a native of California. His grandparents came to the U.S. via England and Chile. My father always said I was one eighth Spanish because his grandmother came from Spain, or so I remember. I recall being taunted by the other children and called a Mexican. I did not know what that meant, but I knew that wasn't me because we were Spanish. It was not until my mother died in 2000, and I was sorting out the things in the house that I ran across an obituary about my great grandmother, Maria Mercedes Webster. It said she was a native of Chile. What a surprise!

This revelation brought to light several bits of information about my father that had gone unnoticed. He had artistic talent in that he liked to paint, take photographs, and write creatively. In purchasing artwork for our home he bought paintings by Latin artists. He made a scrapbook of photos and drawings of his early relationship with my mother, and on the cover of this scrapbook it said "Caramba" with a picture of a man who had fallen off a donkey. Also his secretary was a young Mexican woman of whom he was very supportive. I had never thought about these seemingly unrelated facts before, but now it was making perfect sense. When it came time to study language in school I had no choice in the matter; of course I would study Spanish.

Oh, how I wish that my father were alive and I could ask him some questions about our background! Putting the pieces together in my mind, I believe there was an element of shame connected with his Latin background and some attempt to cover it up. If you saw a picture of my father you could see the Latin heritage and also in me, especially when I was a child. He did say that the Websters on his mother's side of the family were distantly related to Daniel Webster, the statesman.

I never met my paternal grandparents, because they were deceased before I was born. My mother said that my grandfather was the quietest man she had ever met. By that time he had become an alcoholic because he had worked as a bartender all his life. I remember only two stories about my grandmother. First she was Catholic, although I don't think she went to church that often, but she did send my father. He told the story of when she would send him to church, and he would sneak off with his friends and go to the local swimming hole. The other story I remember was about his mother wearing knickers and riding her bicycle. I am sure this was rather unconventional behavior for a young woman around the turn of the twentieth century.

My mother was born and raised in Indiana. She was the oldest of five living children. There was a difference of seventeen years between her and her youngest brother. My mother was a twin and the runt. After she was born, everyone said that this child did not stand a chance to live. The next day another child was born, and this child was much larger, but she died because of too much exposure to whatever anesthetic they used in those days. They had no idea that my grandmother was carrying twins when she gave birth to the second child. So my mother had forces of death coming against her at birth, but God prevailed. She survived against all odds; however, she was sickly as a child and had pneumonia several times.

When she was five she was sent off on foot to the one room schoolhouse that was about a mile and a half away. She was supposed to meet with other children and walk with them, but one day she missed them, and she was too scared to walk by herself so she returned home only to be given a beating by my grandfather. My mother caught pneumonia that winter and was in bed for several months. She always believed that God was punishing her for being a bad girl. It is sad when we make God into some mean, scary person who carries a big stick and punishes us because we are too afraid to walk to school alone at age five!

My mother was raised with her uncle who was about the same age as she. His mother, my great-grandmother, abandoned him when she ran off with another man. So my grandmother raised her brother as her son. The family never spoke ill of my great-grandmother because her husband, my great-grandfather, had a drinking problem. This was common knowledge, so they had compassion for my great-grandmother.

My grandmother was a good Baptist her whole life. There were godly people on my grandfather's side of the family also. His father's name was Elijah, and he had a twin brother, Elisha. It would be difficult to live up to those names, but someone in the family knew their Bible.

In her teen years my mother was a musician. She played the saxophone, and took lessons from the man who was the director of the praise band at the church where she and her family attended. She was on the praise team in addition to playing with her pianist friend for the silent movies. Her teacher, this supposedly godly man, "made a pass" at my mother, and from that time on she would not step into a church.

My mother was ninety years old before she ever mentioned to me that a friend of her father's had molested her. She had been watching Oprah Winfrey about child molestation, and she never thought it had any significance in her life. She had never told anyone about it. Her comment was that her father would have killed the man had he known. I have learned a lot about spiritual dynamics, and I would say that this early experience of sexual victimization probably set her up for the unfortunate experience with her music teacher.

My mother had a reputation of being a party girl; she liked a good time, drinking and dancing. She married her first husband who was many years her senior because he was established, had a good job, and could show her a good time. This was during or right after the Great Depression and an older man with a job was a good catch. She said that after they married he lost interest in going to the nightclubs in Indianapolis, and life with him became boring. When her married girlfriend visited from California, she asked if she could ride out to California with her. So just like that, my mother up and left her husband! As an aside, his first wife had abandoned him also, so we can see how patterns often are repeated. Some would refer to that as a curse.

So off she went to California and settled in Bakersfield, as that is where her friend lived. There she met my father while working as a bookkeeper for an insurance company. My father was one of the traveling agents who came to Bakersfield on his route. There was an office policy that you could not date the agents, so when she changed jobs she informed my father that she could now go out with him. Although

5

she dated him she also had another boyfriend, and when she returned to Indiana to finally get her divorce, she had not decided which man she would marry. She said she believed that my father could give her a better future. For someone who had been poor all her life and had worked during the Great Depression to help support her family, money was always a practical consideration for her.

Mother was twenty-eight and weighed ninety-eight pounds when she married my father; Dad was thirty-two. They were married by a judge in San Francisco and had their wedding dinner at the famous Cliffhouse. They were married forty-eight years before my father died.

My parents settled in Fresno, California, and for the first four years of marriage my mother traveled with my father on his job. They had a grand time in San Francisco, and it remained a tradition in our family that we would go to San Francisco once a year to eat fine food and go to the theatre.

They had trouble conceiving me, and I was told that my father took testosterone shots to assist in the process. My mother was thirty-two and my Dad thirty-eight when I was born. This was considered to be old back in the 40's. I was an Rh baby, which meant that my mother was in the fifteen percent of women whose blood type was Rh negative. In truth there was a blood incompatibility between my mother and me. Part of the family history and a story that I grew up with was that my pediatrician had just been to a conference where he had learned about the Rh factor, and he was able to recognize it; therefore my life was spared. There was another child born the same time as I, and this child was also an Rh baby and he died. My mother and I were quite different in our personalities, and I have often thought the Rh blood factor was an expression of that incompatibility.[1]

My mother said I was yellow and had a pointed head when I was born, and they wanted to send me back to where I came from. That was a family joke because I never doubted that I was a wanted child. The spirit of death that threatened my mother's life at birth was transferred to me, and needless to say, both of us are survivors.

I was born in 1941 during the Second World War. I have pondered the significance of this, and I believe that it must have opened the door to fear. My father traveled for an insurance company, and he was away from home Monday through Friday of every week. My mother stayed home with me. Because we lived in California, there were "brown outs" every night, and my mother was often alone with me. I know that there were times when she was just plain scared. One of those nights she said I was screaming at the top of my lungs, and out of her frustration and fear she hit me across the back. It knocked the wind out of me. I was quiet after that, and she was afraid that she had injured me.

My father doted upon me, but because he left every Monday morning and didn't come back until Friday evening, I believe I grew up feeling abandoned. I can remember when the headlights of his car turned into the driveway on Friday and how excited I was to see him, but I do not ever remember seeing him leave

---

[1] Recently I discovered the possible spiritual roots to Rh incompatibility according to the research department at Be in Health™. I was shocked to see how accurate they were: generational abandonment or rejection by a mother; fear of abandonment and rejection; generational fear, stress, and anxiety; spirits of death and destruction.

on Monday. I was the apple of his eye. He kept a journal of my every move up to the age of six, and after he died my mother presented it to me. What a wonderful gift!

This journal was handwritten in pencil on scraps of paper. As my father's handwriting was worse than most doctors', I asked my mother to please type it for me. At age seventy-six she typed his journal and presented it to me for Christmas with a note that said she would not take a thousand dollars to do it again. The following are a few excerpts:

Around age two:

- Another thing that seems odd is her fear of a balloon. Uncle Joe handed her one to hold while he went for elastic to seal it. She evidently let the air out and it startled her; now she won't have anything to do with it. She is actually afraid of it. We've gotten her over the trembling stage, and she is developing a curiosity though she will not touch it herself. I expect in a short time we will overcome this fear.

- About cocktail time Marcia wants music on the radio so she can dance. She gets her teddy bear and hugs it cheek to cheek, holding one of its paws out at arm's length and proceeds to almost keep time to the music, in forward and backward steps that would pass for dancing, that is, in any place not inhabited by jitterbugs.

- Last weekend I had shown Marcia a picture of Hitler, and she responded, "ba man Itler". When the radio plays Praise the Lord and Pass the Ammunition she always recognizes the tune and starts goose-stepping around the room saying "Praise Ord," something we taught her.

- When I arrived home on Friday she came running to the garage, fast as her tiny legs would carry her, crying "Daddy show sompin! Show sompin!" The sompin was the dining room all decorated for her birthday party. The party was a huge success; she was almost overcome with joy and excitement when all her little friends and their mothers sang "Happy Birthday to you." She was so impressed she almost cried. All day today she has been singing "Happy Birthday You."

- She can also boast. (Pardon me for feeling proud.) The other day when I came home she was in her room playing with Gretchen, a little playmate about her age. I gave her a hello kiss and received in return a trifle more ardent than usual hug around the neck. Then she turned to Gretchen and said, "This is my Daddy, MY DADDY." Gretchen said, "I know."

- Now she is learning Christmas hymns. Much to our delight she gets her book out and starts singing, mixing up the words from different songs. We haven't recognized a tune yet. Her singing goes something like this: "Harka herald angels sing, gloree to the new born king. I like you newborn king! Johnnie get your gun in a cabaret drinking beer was I havin fun."

At age three:

- Marcia at dinner said, "Daddy! Take your hand off the table, it's polite to hold it in your lap."

- Fools and children tell the truth. It had to come out eventually. Our Aunt Ida, who came to visit us, hadn't been in the house a half an hour when our dear little daughter told her, "Aunt Ida, Daddy says you talk an arm off a him."

Christmas 1944:

- Marcia saw Santa Claus for the first time today. After dancing school Mother took she and Karen to the school where Karen's mother was teaching and Santa was visiting. Marcia was deeply impressed, a little shy, and she declined to shake hands with Santa. She accepted an orange and a box of colored crayons and remembered to say, "Thank you." When she got home she told her mother that Santa forgot to say, "You're welcome." That evening she gave me all the details, among which, without a hint of disillusionment, she informed me that Santa had a "fause face" and "there was nothing around here" indicating the place where a rim of white fur should have been according to the pictures she had seen of him. "Santa wasn't very fat."   No criticism, mind you, just an honest observation. This was Marcia's second visit to school; both were extremely happy occasions.   She looks forward with great anticipation to being old enough to go to school.

At age four:

- Marcia: "Is grandma your mother, Mama?"
  Faye: "Yes."
  Marcia: "Where's Daddy's mother?"
  Daddy: "She's not living."
  Marcia: "Where is she?"
  Daddy: "She's in heaven."
  Marcia: "Why?"
  Daddy: "That's a long story, eat your dinner."
  Marcia: "Tell me I can eat and hear!"

Around age four:

- Marcia has a few favorite ties she will ask me to wear when she catches me dressing. Today she picked one that to me seemed a bit wrong for the shirt. We discussed the subject of blend and contrast and to prove my point I picked out a tie that I thought looked best.   Then we went into the living room, displayed both ties and the shirt I was about to put on and asked the advice of mother and Aunt Elizabeth, who was visiting at the time.   Both in unison selected the tie Marcia had picked.   This gave me a laugh when I explained what had happened.

Marcia's prayer at age five:

- Father, Mother, God, loving me
Guard me while I sleep
Guide my little feet up to Thee
I am God's perfect child
Now God I mean it.
Help me to eat well. (I was underweight.)
Help me to be brave when I am hurt
And to help others when they are hurt.
God bless Sally, Connie, Donna and Danny and
God bless Mother and Daddy

At age five and one half:

- Faye was ill and I got breakfast. After much asking where is that and how much of this; some of the answers were furnished by Marcia. At breakfast:

    Marcia: "Daddy, you should stick around more and find out how we do things."

    Daddy: "We got along today O.K. didn't we?"

    Marcia: "Yes, but the day isn't over yet!"

At age six:

- Marcia was given a talking to for doing something "bad."

    Daddy: "Even if we wouldn't have known, if you had not been caught, it's just as naughty. You should never do anything you can't tell your Daddy about. Remember God sees you."

    Marcia: "Well, God made me do it too."

    Daddy: "No He didn't; it's the Devil that makes you do such things."

My parents' lifestyle revolved around evening cocktails, and they both smoked cigarettes. My father's journal documented this and how I would participate with them having my Coke cocktail. Also I

11

learned to pantomime striking a match on my shoe, lighting a cigarette and smoking it.

I think I could say that I was somewhat precocious. I spoke my mind at an early age and was a keen observer of my environment. My parents let me express my opinion as I was growing up. I think this was because I was an only child and because my mother was not allowed to express her opinion to her mother. I spent a lot of time with the adults, as I was not sent to my room because of company. I did not like it when we visited others who had children, and the children would be made to go into another room. I felt as if I were missing something, and being relegated to another room seemed like punishment.

I began dancing at an early age. My mother put me into a tap dancing class. I remember my first recital. A group of us stood in a line on stage and sang "Twinkle, Twinkle Little Star." The girl next to me cried her way through the entire performance. I did not understand why she would do such a thing. I loved to dance and sing, and an audience did not intimidate me. I continued to take dance lessons for the next five years.

As my father was a Catholic and my mother was a Baptist, they had an agreement not to discuss or argue about religion. So I went to church with a neighbor child who lived across the street. She attended Christian Science Sunday school. This was not quite so far out as it might seem, as I had a great aunt who was a Christian Scientist. This was my first formal religious teaching. When I visited Boston at age sixty-three and drove by the Christian Science mother church, I recognized it from having seen a picture of it in Sunday school. One summer I attended a two-week Bible school at a Presbyterian church. We memorized the books of the Bible, and I still have in my possession a small card that listed the books of the Bible that was given to me in that class.

One thing I looked forward to was our annual vacation time in San Francisco. I would stay with my great aunt, and my parents would stay in a hotel. My Aunt Ida lived just a couple of blocks from Union Square, and she and I would walk there in the morning to sit and visit with her cronies. In the afternoon she would curl my hair with a curling iron. This was a totally new experience for me, and I felt so special. My mother braided my hair in French braids, and it was an unpleasant and painful time for me with much complaining. I remember hearing the clanging of the cable cars as they made their way up the hill from my aunt's apartment. Those were good times.

My childhood was happy even though I was somewhat lonely. I was especially lonely on Sunday mornings because my parents often had a hangover, and they would want to sleep late. Even when I was in college I would have a recurring depression every Sunday. Perhaps I was longing for church, but it probably was programming from the past.

Marcia at age 5
1946

Chapter Two

School Days

I entered kindergarten at the tender age of four and one half. I took the bus to school with other children, but because I got out early, I had to return home by myself. One time a man at the bus stop stalked me. I told my parents and the teacher. The next day the teacher sent me off to the bus stop two blocks away in a tree-lined residential neighborhood. It seemed dark and scary because of all the trees. Little did I know that my father was parked across the street watching my every move. I was fine and the man did not reappear. Was he there in the first place or did my fear produce him?

My first grade teacher said on my report card, "Marcia works independently, but often disturbs her neighbors by visiting during school." My second grade teacher said, "Talks too much." In the second grade I was a little slow in learning to read, and I had to attend a tutorial class. In the fourth grade I was one of the teacher's pets, and that positive attention was a boon to my grades. By the sixth grade I was selected as citizen of the week.

My parents took me to all the movies made for children. I remember being so traumatized by *Lassie Come Home* that I had to be removed from the theater because I was crying so loudly. I could not see an animal being hurt without becoming hysterical. As an adult I have watched those old movies and have seen what a good actor Lassie was.   He was acting, but it seemed real to me!

The seventh grade began junior high school. Quite by accident I made mostly A's and a couple of B's. Physical Education was usually the class in which I earned a B. The second semester of eighth grade I earned straight A's. Strange as this may seem, it became a problem. I became driven to achieve good grades, more than good, straight A's to be exact. This continued throughout high school. I discovered that this was a way I could gain recognition, and because I was not very popular otherwise, it was an avenue through which I gained positive attention.

I had two, maybe three, major disappointments in high school. I wanted more than anything to become a pom-pom girl. This was an honor reserved for upper classmen. Always in the past the contestants were judged on their ability. The year I became eligible they changed the rules. We had tryouts and I made it to the finals. I had been dancing since the age of four, and I knew I was good and had a chance. But this year they had the student body vote on whom they liked the best. It became a popularity contest, and I did not win. This broke my heart. I thought it was so unfair because you could not win on ability alone.

Socially, I was a little backward. I had a few close friends but no serious boyfriends. I did not attend any of my proms. I remember loaning out my clothes to my friend who was popular, so that she could go to the dances.

By this time my mother was concerned that I was spending too much time studying and not enough time socializing. I know she wanted the best for me; however, she was not interested in intellectual pursuits, and I never knew her to read a book unless it was a *Readers' Digest Condensed Book.* I took after my father who was an avid reader. My favorite thing for summer vacation was to go to the library and check out some novels and stay up practically all night reading.

My father was a quiet man, and my mother ran the household, but she did it in the name of my father. It was always - your father wants you to do this or that. I was generally a good girl, and if my father said it, I would do it. To this day, with both of them deceased, I do not know if she said that to manipulate me or if it was really his desire. It was certainly consistent with how I knew him to be.

My mother was the social one while my Dad was the introvert. I grew up hearing, "You are just like your father." It sounded like some kind of indictment. I really did not know what she meant, but I knew it was not a compliment.

By the time I was seven years old, my father had purchased his own business selling insurance. Now he was home seven nights a week, however, he was a workaholic and did not get home until later in the evening. By three o'clock in the afternoon the social hour had begun with my mother and her friends. I had my dinner by myself, usually around six at a card table in front of the TV. My mother would have a few more cocktails with my father when he got home, and they would eat around nine. That habit of eating alone carries over to today; I still eat my dinner in front of the TV, often watching the national news.

My mother would criticize me for going into my room and closing the door when she had her friends over in the afternoon. After she had a few drinks she would tell me that I was unsociable and had no friends. I, of course, did not agree, but it hurt anyway. I was really going into my room to get away from the drinking because I had developed a hatred of it, and I did not like to be around it. When she would start her tirade I knew exactly what she was going to say, so I would finish the sentences for her, saying that I had no friends and no one liked me. In this way I was controlling the accusation, and supposedly, it was less hurtful. I did not understand that I was speaking a curse over myself and that I had let in a spirit of self-rejection.

Frequently when my mother had been drinking, she would become homesick for her family in Indiana. I used to think, are we not a family? What is wrong with us, that we are not enough for you? All her life my mother referred to Indiana as home even though she lived in California for over sixty years.

Although I continued to make excellent grades, it was not something that my parents showed appreciation for. They were never as excited about my A's as I was. The drive to excel came from within me and was not something my parents motivated.

I disapproved of my parents' lifestyle so much that, when I started smoking at age seventeen, I hid it from them. I don't think it would have mattered, but I could not give them the satisfaction. I only smoked in my bedroom when they were not at home. I was foolish enough to think they would not smell the smoke, and if they did, they never said anything.

I had a framed picture on the wall of my bedroom that depicted a man crouched down in a box with a scowl on his face. The caption read, "People are no damned good." Mother did not approve of this picture either, but it expressed my anger and rebellion at that age.

I remember getting drunk only one time in my life. I was with my high school boyfriend in my living room. We drank a large bottle of cheap, red table wine in the presence of my father who was reading in the same room. This was rather typical of my father to be oblivious to what was happening around him when lost in a book. I became dizzy and nauseous from the wine and so disliked the sensation of my consciousness being altered by alcohol, that I never got drunk again.

The second event that represented a major loss to me, after not becoming a pom-pom girl, was not getting into the college of my choice. I continued to make excellent grades, and I graduated fourth in my class of over six hundred. I decided that I wanted to go to Stanford University; however, I am not entirely sure why. Some of the reasons I may have chosen it were: the prestige, my best friend also wanting to go there, and the great ratio of boys to girls. My mother used to say, "You don't need to go to college; you are just going to get married." I proved her wrong; I never married. In retrospect, I can see that much of my young adult life was spent in rebellion against my mother.

In any case, Stanford did not accept me; they accepted four from my class, three girls and one boy: the valedictorian of my class, my best friend, a boy who was ninth or tenth in the class, and a girl whose qualification was that her father was a graduate of Stanford. It seemed so unjust! I had spent the last seven years of my life striving to earn the best possible grades and for what? My heart was broken. My second choice of schools was the University of California in Berkeley. I had several college friends telling me what a fantastic school Cal was and every bit as good as Stanford. It was small consolation. I often wondered what my life would have been like had I gone to Stanford. Would I have married perhaps? I would never know.

I was brought up under a protestant work ethic, and I thought that by doing well, excelling, being good, etc. I would be rewarded, just as many believe that they can earn their way into heaven through good works. I still catch myself living as such, but I have been shown many times that it is not what you do, but who you are and how much you are liked, and whom you know and who knows you. Relationship is what is important: relationship with God, relationship with yourself, and relationship with others. The important question is, "Are you known of God?"

Marcia and Sandra in front of the galleria
Milan, Italy 1960

Chapter Three

Living in Italy

I entered the University of California at Berkeley in the fall of 1958. I registered too late to be accepted into the dorms so unless I wanted to live independently, I had to join a sorority. Rushing was another difficult experience to endure. It certainly reinforces rejection and painfully points out the lack of social skills needed to make one popular. I was the brainy one who didn't even attend her prom. But I did pledge a sorority, and I met a girl who was to become a good friend. Sandra was another high achiever who had entered college a year early because of her intelligence. Her parents lived in Berkeley, and I became acquainted with her family. Later, I experienced a great time living with them in Italy.

I enjoyed being a part of a large student body where I could lose myself, and no one really knew who I was. I thought I would major in chemistry, but after taking Chemistry IA and getting a C, I quickly changed my mind and decided to major in the humanities. I thoroughly enjoyed my studies of history, literature, art and music.

And I soon discovered folk dancing. Sandra and I folk danced every Friday night at the Senior Men's Hall, a log cabin in the woods on campus. We made many friends that were not of the sorority/fraternity crowd. We had a girlfriend from Austria, and I made friends with a man who was a Moroccan Jew. God has put into my heart a love for people from other nations. Whether it came from my Chilean ancestry or rebellion against my parents and their lifestyle, I don't know. It was probably a little of both. We also danced on the lawn outside the gym at lunchtime and sat on the grass. This was much to the consternation of our sorority sisters. One of the rules was that as young ladies we were not supposed to sit on the grass.

The cultural influence during the late 50's was the beatnik generation, thriving across the bay in San Francisco. Black clothes and black tights were in. On Telegraph Ave. in Berkeley there existed a coffee shop that served cappuccino and other strong coffees. This is where the radicals hung out. I wore a lot of black, much to my mother's disapproval. I would dress up in my black sweater, black straight skirt and black tights and go to the coffee shop and pretend that I belonged with the radical intellectuals. I also loved foreign movies with subtitles that played in small artsy theaters in the Bay Area. Once my boyfriend from Fresno came to visit, and we saw four different foreign movies on the same day, all at different theaters.

In the fall of our sophomore year, Sandra's stepfather was sent to Italy to work for an Italian company that was doing research on the first synthetic fabrics that could be made into clothes. Sandra and her mother accompanied him. It had been a long time dream of mine to go to Europe, and I had begun to collect information about schools that had a semester abroad. But even much better, Sandra's parents invited me to come to Milan and spend the spring semester with them. Unfortunately I came down with mononucleosis that fall semester, having caught the "kissing disease" from the man I was dating. My liver was enlarged, and for the first time I developed allergies. I remember sleeping through almost the entire fall semester. I still earned straight B's.

My father gave me permission to go to Europe only if I purchased a return ticket in advance, and I promised that I would return on that date. He had friends whose children went to Europe and never did come back. I accepted his conditions and promised to return; so on Feb. 2, 1960, I boarded a Pan American flight leaving San Francisco for London.

I remember the thrill of that plane taking off. It was probably my first jet airplane ride. The engines roared so loudly I could not hear myself think, and gravity threw me back against the headrest. Oh, how exciting it was when that plane lifted off the ground. My dream was being fulfilled. I was nineteen and I had achieved my life goal. What was next?

We were a little late arriving in London, and I missed my connection to Milan. There I was in a foreign country, nineteen years old and by myself. I sent my friends an urgent telegram telling them I missed the flight and would arrive at 10 p.m. There was a Chinese gentleman who walked with a decided limp and spoke very broken English, and he was also making the same connection. His name was Mr. Fung. I attached myself to him, and he took me under his wing until we landed in Milan. Mr. Fung was a merchant seaman who had an Italian wife in Genoa; he was going to visit her. I thank the Lord for Mr. Fung because I was one of the only females on the flight from London to Milan, and in 1960 it was not safe for a woman to be traveling alone at night in Italy.

The months I spent in Italy were some of the happiest times in my life. I loved the European lifestyle. I immersed myself in Italian culture, and Milan became Milano. My friends had an apartment on Corso Sempione in the fashionable Milano. My room was actually the maid's quarters. I had to go outside onto the *terrazzo* and climb up narrow stairs to a small room that contained a single bed and a small sink. That was my haven. In the morning I would awaken to the sounds of the maids or housewives beating their rugs over the banister of their *terrazzo*. That's the Italian way of cleaning and freshening.

I made notes on my first bus ride in Milano. There is an art to it that had to be learned in order to survive. One enters the back door between mobs of people pushing each other. It cost six cents; I'm sure it is more today. There are very few seats so the majority of the people have to stand. The handrails are overhead; they are difficult to reach for anyone who is short, and that described me. The game is to work your way to the front of the bus in time to get off at your stop. The people are jam-packed in, and the migration to the front is achieved by aggressive pushing. Occasionally someone will say excuse me, but not often. The women were the most aggressive pushers. The bus stops very fast, and everyone *en masse* falls forward trying to catch themselves. Then the bus is off again. By the time we got back home I had learned to push and could hold my own. All this was a game and fun for me, although Sandra did not agree.

With my dark hair I blended in with the Italians, but Sandra with her height and blond hair stood out. She attracted a lot of attention, especially from the opposite sex, because she was different. We would be walking down the street and people would yell, "Tedesche!" meaning Germans in Italian. We would shout back "No, Americane!" They hated the Germans because of WW II, but loved the Americans because we helped liberate Italy.

We ate dinner every night at a local *trattoria*, which is a small family restaurant. There were two American men who also patronized the "trot" as we called it. Tom and James were opera students. Also there were two young Italian men from the neighborhood with whom we became friends. The proprietor's daughter, Maria, enjoyed our company. She took us dancing, or "ballare," when I had been there only about a week. Once the young men realized we were American, they all wanted to dance with us. I did not know a word of Italian at that point. It made for an interesting evening of fending off unwanted attention and listening to conversation that didn't make any sense. They all talked about their "macchina." I later learned that was their car.

I kept a diary and I wrote down something that Maria said about me. She said that when I first arrived I was very quiet and plain looking, but after being in Italy for a while I became talkative and pretty. And Italy got all the credit. I think God had something to do with it.

We traveled throughout most of Europe from Scandinavia to Portugal to Yugoslavia and Greece and everything in between. We traveled by boat, car and train. Sometimes Sandra's mother traveled with us, but most of the time it was Sandra and I traveling alone. I even went to a few places on my own. It was a wonderful time to be in Europe. It was a time of innocence before the sexual revolution and the advent of feminism. We would often have live music on the train from our fellow travelers. Many a night on the train we would be singing into the wee hours. Once we even danced down the aisle with some Yugoslav students.

Our dream came true when we visited Yugoslavia. As folk dancers, our favorite dances came from the Balkans. We visited every Ethnographic museum we could find. We went to the outdoor markets and chased after peasants in order to photograph their native dress. We purchased several authentic costumes including beautiful, floor length Croatian dresses with long sleeves and aprons. They were made out of heavy linen with beautiful, brightly colored flowers embroidered in satin with cutwork lace.

The hours some woman must have spent making those dresses by hand made them invaluable. We had to get governmental permission to take these costumes out of the country. In 1960 the peasants wore their native dress to the market or to work in the fields. In the open markets when we inquired about what someone was wearing, there would appear many people out of nowhere asking us to buy their costume pieces.

After returning to Milan we received a telegram inviting us to join Sokoli, a group in San Francisco that exhibited folk dances from the Balkans. Another dream come true. We were sophomores in college and this was a group of adults older than ourselves; it was an honor to be asked to dance with them.

Chapter Four

Communist Experience

In the summer shortly before returning to the U.S., Sandra and I went to Scandinavia by train. It was a wonderful trip until we started our return to Italy. We wanted to visit Berlin on the way home. We had inquired about travel to Berlin while in Milano before leaving; however, the unanimous advice we were given was to fly. We said no, we wanted to take the train. However, no one was able to give us information about ground transportation.

We purchased our tickets for Berlin in Copenhagen. We left by train and when we got to the channel we got off and entered a small ferryboat headed for East Germany. This was most definitely off the beaten track for Americans. The sea was quite rough that day. Paper bags were being distributed to the passengers, and I thought I might need one. This whole day had been confusing and a little frightening because we never really knew what we were doing or where we were going. And worst of all, no one spoke English. We finally met a German woman who could speak both Danish and English. She and her Danish husband were going to Berlin, so we asked if we could follow them. We purchased a visa for Berlin on the ferryboat.

When we got to East Germany we were herded off the boat and into the train station. We finally found the train to Berlin, a strange little train with only two cars. We were told that we couldn't board without seat reservations. We had inquired about this in

Copenhagen, but were told that it was impossible to reserve seats. After much conversation that was all in German, we were allowed to board. As all the seats were taken in second class, we were allowed into the first class without having to pay extra. This train was very fast and made very few stops. No one was allowed off the train until it arrived in East Berlin. Thank God for the German woman who helped us, as I don't know how we would have found our way. East Berlin was so stark and without life; it was very depressing. We took the S Bahn, an elevated railway into West Berlin. Our friend telephoned around and found a hotel for us and gave us directions about how to find it from the station. We spent a couple of days seeing the sights both in West and East Berlin. This was before the Berlin Wall had been built, and you could take public transportation between the different parts of the city.

We had spent almost all our money when we were ready to return to Milano. We purchased food for the train that left at 7:45 p.m. We enjoyed our ride for about an hour before we stopped for the border guard. Our car was in the middle of the train, and as they were working from both ends it took them a while to get to us. The guard started to look at my passport, and I could tell immediately that something was wrong. After discussion among themselves they said to Sandra and me, "You have no visa. 'Nix visem.' You must leave the train and return to Berlin." We were aghast. We got our visa for exit on the boat coming into East Germany, or so we thought. It didn't matter; we had to leave the train to be stranded, who knows where, in East Germany. When we got off the train, it left the station. Sandra was tearful. I was very nervous and upset but remained a little calmer. One of the policemen spoke English, and he was kind enough to explain that we had purchased a visa that was good for twenty-four hours, but we had stayed longer. When we purchased the visa no one spoke English, so we did not know what we were getting.

The policeman who spoke English was very nice and polite. He explained everything to us and tried not to frighten us anymore than we already were. He was very helpful and gave us the address in East Berlin where we could buy another visa. Because the next day was Sunday we were going to be stranded with very little funds until we could leave on Monday. We were told that someone would give us a ride back to Berlin. In the meantime, he took our passports and told us to sit on the red bench. I don't know the significance of the red bench, but all the benches were green except one red one, and there we sat. It was quite cold and we sat there for a very long time. We had to wait until all the trains for the night had passed through. There were at least ten border guards, and they all seemed to be amused by our plight. Finally, after some time, all the policemen left. That scared us even more as we thought we were going to be stranded.

Our English-speaking friend returned and told us it would be another half hour and disappeared again. We weren't alone as three soldiers arrived. One carried a rifle and another had our passports in his hand. I think they were guarding us. Much later, the police arrived with two German women who were very frightened. Apparently they had also done something wrong. Finally we were told to come along. The soldiers carried our luggage for us, and we were led to an army truck. The two German women got into the front cab, and we were hoisted into the back end with the soldiers and the policemen. The truck was the military type with the benches on each side and with a canvas top. Well, there we sat with all the German soviets riding off into the night to God knows where. The policemen were very good-natured and seemed to be happy. We did not have far to go to where we were left off at the S Bahn station.

Our passports were returned to us and we were put on the train headed for Berlin. We arrived back in Berlin at around midnight, nervous but safe. Our next problem was finding a hotel. We were exhausted and I refused to walk, so we took a taxi. We found a hotel that had a room in the "garden house" which turned out to be a room under the S Bahn train tracks, so we heard every train that passed.

We learned that you could purchase a visa at any of the legal crossing points, but if you planned to stay more than twenty-four hours, you had to go into East Berlin to obtain an exit visa. One could fly in and out without any problem, but because we were traveling through Communist territory you had to have an exit visa. They allowed only ten trains a day in and out of Berlin. There was no telephone connection between East and West Berlin. The S Bahn, which was Soviet operated, was one of the few means of transportation connecting these sections of Berlin.

On Sunday we were feeling anti-Berlin, anti-sightseeing, anti-everything. We spent the afternoon in a sidewalk café drinking Coke and watching the Germans promenade the sidewalks. Later we found the only English-speaking movie in town, which was *Porgy and Bess*.

On Monday we took the S Bahn to East Berlin and had a long walk to the building where the visas were issued. The forms were in German, Danish and Swedish, none of which we could read. Our cameras had to be checked, and we were sent upstairs. We entered a large smoke-filled room where many people were waiting. There were German magazines to read. We found one in French that Sandra could read on the advantages of collective farming. We were given a number and had to wait our turn. We waited for about two hours to get our visa. Now we had a visa good for another twenty-four hours, and we were able to leave Berlin that evening. Everything went smoothly at the border. The guard recognized us, and we recognized him; but he did not acknowledge us, or we him. To add insult to injury, Sandra's suitcase was stolen off the train. We got off in Zurich to report it and missed our connection, so we did not get into Milano until after midnight, thoroughly exhausted.

In September we returned to the United States. I was so sad to leave Italy, and I definitely wanted to stay longer, but because of the promise I made to my father I returned to resume school. Orson Wells was on our flight, but I could not have cared less as I was so distraught about leaving. I remember giving our American friend James a big hug and holding on to him so tight as if to say, "Don't let me go." He was startled and didn't know what to do with me. It is difficult to explain how you can feel more at home in a foreign county than you do in your own land. I love the extroversion of the Italians, the flamboyant way they express themselves. I have felt too repressed in America. People who know me might find this strange, since I tend to be quiet.

Marcia wearing Korean national dress
1962

Chapter Five

First Love

Sandra and I entered back into university life. In spite of the activities in school I felt lonely and depressed and missed Italy. This time I studied Italian. I even took a class on Dante's *Divina Comedia* taught in Italian! And we were dancing with Sokoli in San Francisco, but I developed painful shin splints and had to sit out most of the year.

I remember the first time I saw a belly dancer. We had been to a Sokoli rehearsal, and afterward everyone wanted to go to this small bar in the neighborhood and listen to some oud music. The oud is a popular stringed instrument from the Middle East. Sandra and I were underage, but we sneaked in unnoticed. A woman stood up at the urging of her companions, and she began to dance a solo. She was dressed in a plain black sheath dress, and her hair was up in a bun. She began taking her hair down in a most sensual manner while dancing. I thought it was the most beautiful dance I had ever seen. It made a strong imprint in my memory.

It was also during this time that another college friend of mine introduced me to the pendulum; this was my formal introduction into an occult activity. Someone had taught her how to ask questions and wait for the pendulum to start moving. She asked the pendulum if she was going to have children. If the pendulum moved to the right, the answer was yes, and if it moved to the left, it was no. The answer for her was yes. When I asked the pendulum the same question, it moved to the left. I immediately became fearful. We repeated the exercise several times, and it was always the same. We had opened the door to divination just as if we had played with an ouji board. And this prediction came to pass. Scripture says in Job 3:25 that what Job feared the most came upon him. In psychology they call this phenomena a self-fulfilling prophecy. I never forgot that little exercise; it would come back to haunt me over the years.

The following summer I registered for summer school to make up some of the credits I missed while I had mononucleosis and while I was in Italy. I moved into International House for the summer. The first weekend we had a welcome dance. I had made a promise to myself that I would not get involved with any Persian or Arab students. So when a Korean friend of mine, whom I had met in a dancing class, introduced me to another Korean man, I was caught totally off guard. That evening began a four-year relationship with Mr. Park. Koreans always say their last name first before their given name, so Park was how I referred to him.

He was very handsome and quite talented. He had a beautiful singing voice, and he was an excellent dancer. Foreign students at the University of California at Berkeley were exceptional students and from good families that could afford to send their children abroad. Park was also an excellent soccer player and became the captain of the team. I had never been to a soccer game in my life, but I soon attended them all. The team was quite international, as soccer was not yet popular among Americans. He became All American center forward. This is always an honor, but more so because Cal was not known for its athletes and had too few All Americans.

Because Park had always said he would return to Korea, I knew that I would not marry him. Korean culture was something that interested me, but it was not something that I could live in. We spent many hours visiting with his friends, that is, his male friends. When we visited his closest friend, the wife would serve us refreshments and then disappear into another part of the house with her sister. In Korean homes there are separate living areas for the men and the women. As an American woman I was allowed to socialize with the men. They would switch back and forth from Korean to English so I could understand some of the conversation. Park had one Korean friend whose wife was Chinese. She also remained and joined in the conversation when we visited them. She was not well received by the other Koreans because she was Chinese.

His friends treated me with respect, but I felt somewhat invisible. I remember a New Year's Eve party where a European woman and I were the only Caucasians present. She became very upset because she felt ignored by her date, and the Asian women were not friendly to her, but I was used to this separation of the sexes where the men had their own camaraderie, and the Asian women kept to themselves. Language, of course, was also a barrier.

I had many interesting experiences with Park. We had dinner one night with the Korean consulate and his family in San Francisco. I was trying my best not to drop any food with my chopsticks while I served myself from the communal dishes on the table. Everyone is given a bowl of rice, but you had to reach for the other dishes with your chopsticks. I was fairly successful and proud of myself.

Another time we went to a large party for international students in San Francisco. I had frequently been mistaken for being Jewish because of my last name, my small stature, and dark hair. I remember a French woman putting her arm around me and saying, "We Jewish girls have big hips, don't we?" I smiled and nodded yes. At this same party the woman, whom I had seen belly dancing in the bar, was there as a guest, and she was asked to dance. I thought this was some kind of divine providence that I should see her again. In retrospect it may have been an assignment from the enemy to help me move further into the realm of sin.

One of the international fairs at Cal featured a professional belly dancer from a Broadway club in San Francisco. I wanted to talk with her and ask her where I could learn to dance. Park was very supportive and urged me to be bold and go up to her. She gave me the name of a dance teacher whom I later contacted and began learning the art of belly dance.

Finally, I took Park home to meet my family, and they graciously received him. He cooked a Korean dinner for my friends one Christmas when we were in Fresno. In fact, he taught me how to cook some of his favorite food. He was full of herbal folk wisdom that he had learned from his mother, but in the early 1960's herbal medicine had not yet become popular, not even in California.

At age twenty I fell in love with Park and lost my virginity. I had a great deal of shame regarding our sexual relationship. I had somehow come to the conclusion that I should sacrifice myself for this doomed relationship. It was doomed because I knew I would never marry him and move to Korea, but I sacrificed my virginity for love. I sacrificed some of the best years of my youth for this relationship. I even heard comments that no one else would want me because I had been involved with someone of another race. It is amazing that we listen to all the voices in our head and believe their lies.

I was terrified that I would become pregnant. I went to my family doctor in Fresno, and he immediately offered me a prescription for birth control pills. I didn't even know they were available. So I began taking the Pill. Around the same time I developed severe gastrointestinal cramping. The pain would not let up until I emptied my intestines. These pains could hit me any time of the day or night. I was afraid of being sick somewhere where there was no rest room. Would I make it through my exam? Would I be embarrassed and have to excuse myself? For the next eight years of my life I lived with this pain and fear. At times I wished I were dead.

So I was the one to break off the relationship with Park. It was not going anywhere, and I felt burdened by it. Park became very depressed and refused to take his graduate school exams. I felt responsible for this, and I remember phoning the foreign student advisor and confessing to him what had happened. He intervened and convinced Park to take his exams.

Marcia during the "hippy" stage
1971

Chapter Six

Becoming a Hippy

My first job out of college was as an engineer's aid at Chevron Research Corporation. As an art history major I was a little out of my element. I had been on this job for about a year when a friend recommended that I become a social worker for the county. She said it was the easiest job, that all you had to do was talk with people. Since I liked people this seemed like a reasonable thing to pursue. So I began working for the Welfare Department in Aid to Families with Dependent Children. My district was in the West Oakland ghetto. I can still remember the first family I ever visited. The living conditions were appalling, but I was somehow able to adapt myself to whatever the circumstances. I recall how shocked I was that there were no paved sidewalks in West Oakland. How could they have sidewalks in one part of town and not in another? I was so very naïve.

I had not been working very long as a social worker when I came down with what was in reality Hepatitis A, but my doctor in Oakland had not been able to make a proper diagnosis. I had a pain in my right side that was progressively growing worse. He prescribed a tranquilizer to deal with this pain. It finally became so severe that I could hardly walk. At that point I returned home to mother who called our family doctor. He also brushed me off when he saw the medication that had been prescribed. It was finally a nurse who lived next door to us who said, "You had better get that doctor back out here." After a blood test the doctor was very apologetic for not taking me seriously. I supposedly had a mild case of hepatitis, although I had never before been so sick.

I had grown up in a world that was racially singular. Outwardly my parents were not prejudiced, but my father seemed to have more problems in this area than my mother. He objected to a gay male friend of mine from high school, and when I began dating a black man he became very upset. I was a little shocked because they had accepted Park without a problem.

I met Rich at the welfare department; he was one of the other social workers. We became friends and eventually he asked me out. Our first date ended in date rape. I did a very strange thing. Because I could not tolerate any kind of a breach in my heart, I entered into a relationship with him. That was a mistake. My life was tied up for another four years. We even planned to marry, but he backed out saying that he had only promised to marry me because he was afraid of losing me.

All this was happening during the time in history when Black Power was on the rise. It was not the time for a black man to have a white girlfriend in California. There was a lot of hostility toward whites, and I definitely did not think of myself as a "honky." I remember arguing with him and another black friend of his about using the word Negro. I could see nothing wrong with it, and I was arguing my case. Rich had a problem with my being white, and frequently he was concerned that people were looking at us. They probably were, but I paid it no attention. However, after too much time had lapsed I also ended this relationship.

I decided to go back to school to get a graduate degree in social welfare. It was my supervisor at the welfare department who was my inspiration, and both she and I entered Cal at the same time to earn our degrees. My fieldwork placement the first year was at a state mental hospital for the developmentally disabled. During the second year I interned at an out patient psychiatric clinic in San Francisco. This was a prestigious placement known for its loyalty to Freudian psychoanalysis. After graduate school I returned to the welfare department to work off a stipend I had received from the state.

During this time I joined Synanon, an organization that rehabilitated hard-core drug addicts. Synanon was known for its "game" which was a confrontational type of encounter group. Too often they crossed the line of verbal abuse when addressing the person who was on the "hot seat." This organization is no longer in existence. As a square, meaning that I was not a drug addict, I could also play the Synanon game. We were assigned to a tribe, and strange as it may seem, this was a time in my life when I actually felt a part of something, like I belonged. Our tribe was mixed racially and a mixture of addicts and squares. The squares formed a large social group that hung together outside of the organization.

Through some of my Synanon friends I was set up on a blind date with Tom. We were so different. He was burned out because of overuse of psychedelic drugs, and I was a social worker with a master's degree and a professional helper. Tom was six foot six with red hair, and he had a charismatic personality. I had dated him a few times and was falling for him before I learned that he was seven years my junior.

Tom always said I saved his life. He was unemployed, broken-hearted because of separation from two young sons, and having difficulties with his mind and emotions because of drug use. I had a heart of compassion for him. This actually began a string of relationships where I nurtured men who were broken in spirit, soul, and body. It may have been good for them but definitely not good for me. No man will fall in love with the person who mothers him.

Tom moved in with me and I supported him. He introduced me to marijuana, and I remember the first time I got high. We were walking around the university campus, my legs feeling like lead, and my purse weighing a ton. I sat down in the middle of the sidewalk laughing. Tom was trying to get me to behave normally so we would not attract attention, but I couldn't have cared less.

Tom also introduced me to the music of the day: The Rolling Stones, The Who, Pink Floyd, Jimmy Hendrix, etc. He liked Crosby, Stills and Nash, especially Graham Nash's song: "Our house, a very, very fine house with two cats in the yard . . ." So we had to get a cat. This was the first cat I owned as I had grown up with dogs, but this began my affection for cats that exists to this day. Tom named one of my all time favorite cats Mithrander, a name taken from Tolkien's *Lord of the Rings*. I have found it curious that so many Christians relate to these books, because when we were high on drugs we read *The Hobbit*, and *Lord of the Rings* along with Carlos Castaneda's *The Teachings of Don Juan: the Yaqui Way of Knowledge*. Both authors made references to smoke or to drugs that took you into different worlds of altered consciousness; this is evidence that occultism was involved.

I had adopted a hippy lifestyle by now: long hair, braless, the natural look without makeup, ethnic clothes, etc. We purchased a Volkswagen bus and converted the rear into living quarters. I quit my job, and we left in the bus headed for the East Coast where Tom's family lived. We stayed stoned as much as possible and never passed by hitchhikers without picking them up. This was not my choice, as I was made anxious by some of these people. We made our way across the country visiting all the national parks along the way.

We stayed with Tom's family, but his family's life was like nothing I had experienced before. His parents were separated, and his mother was a very unhappy woman. Tom had younger brothers who were rebellious. The boys fought with each other, and there were holes in the wall from their angry fists.

We continued our adventure while driving up through New England to Canada. I became pregnant sometime during this trip, and I was still plagued with the severe intestinal cramping. Tom did not have patience for my physical problems.

On one of our adventures to the World's Trade Fair, I was so high that I thought I was losing my mind. Tom told me he had slipped me some very strong LSD. I had never taken LSD before and was afraid of it, but actually he lied to me, and I was having some kind of reaction to the marijuana we had smoked.

On returning to America from Canada, we were stopped by the police at the border. Because of our hippy appearance, they suspected that we had drugs. Actually Tom had marijuana hidden on his person. They went over the bus with a fine-toothed comb. I remember how they tasted a green herb that was on the floor thinking it was marijuana. Fortunately it turned out to be oregano. I was left alone, but they took Tom away to search him. I was so very frightened that they would find the drugs, and we would be arrested, but we were blessed that they did not find anything, and we were let go.

In addition to my usual gastrointestinal problems, I had been having respiratory symptoms and had gone to the local clinic where I had chest x-rays.

They told me I had walking pneumonia. I returned to California by myself, and it was my own doctor who told me that I was pregnant. My first response was that I wanted to keep the baby, but I was concerned about the exposure to x-rays and the drug use. I thought I would have to raise this child alone because Tom was not someone I could count on. I was amazed at the total lack of support from everyone concerning this child. When I called the doctor's office to find out if I was pregnant the nurse said in the next breath, "Do you want an abortion?" My best friend was insistent that I get an abortion saying that it was irresponsible to raise a child alone. My two former supervisors at the Welfare Department said that I could never return to work as a single parent with an out-of-wedlock child because I worked with single mothers, and it would encourage them to have out-of-wedlock children, which they already had anyway.

I will not justify the abortion with the reasons why, but suffice it to say, I had ungodly thoughts as to why I needed an abortion. I did not consult Tom regarding this decision, but on my own obtained a legal abortion. I was coming against my own will in the situation, and I had to convince a psychiatrist that I would have an emotional breakdown if I did not have the abortion. In my whole life, the abortion is the one act I most deeply regret.

Tom returned to California and we continued to live together pretending to be married for the sake of my job. I eventually began experimenting with LSD and Mescaline. During the first trip I took on psychedelics, I remember not being able to look Tom in the face. There was something about his face that was so frightful. He told me that what I saw was a projection of my own fear; it was in me and not on his face.

Our relationship broke up about six months later when he left me for another woman. They later married and had several children. The breakup of this relationship was devastating to me; it seemed that I cried every day for weeks unable to get past the loss. Tom died in his forties from kidney cancer that may have been connected to his abuse of drugs.

Marcia dancing at a club in Berkeley, CA
1972

Chapter Seven

From Europe to Afghanistan

I continued to live and work in the East Bay. I participated in the local new age culture in Berkeley where I met Jim at an encounter group at the YWCA. He was another hippy with long blond hair. Because of my experience with Tom, I assumed he would be similar in his choice of drugs, but I was mistaken. He was dependent on speed, which is methamphetimine, and I did not become cognizant of this until many months into the relationship.

Jim was a nurse and worked at a convalescent home in San Francisco. We were living together, and he was shooting up with speed every morning in the bathroom, unbeknownst to me. Periodically he would be sick with the "flu" and spend the weekend sleeping. I had no idea that he was crashing from speed, and I would nurse him, rub his back, and cater to his needs. When I discovered he was shooting meth, I felt like a fool because I was the graduate social worker who was supposed to be savvy about these matters.

During these years I continued to study belly dancing. I never thought of performing, as I danced mostly for my own pleasure. However, many other dancers came, learned to dance and then went on stage. I believe it was my competitive spirit, and also some jealousy and envy, that finally I too wanted to dance professionally. My first experience on stage was at a Renaissance Fair in California. I had so much fun dancing; I caught the performance bug. My first job dancing out of town was in Salt Lake City at a Greek restaurant, and Jim went with me on this two-week adventure. Salt Lake City was a unique experience in itself.

The management of this restaurant encouraged me to sit with the customers and allow them to buy me drinks. I told them that I did not want to drink alcohol, and they said that was okay, just order it with Coke, and they would bring me a plain Coke.[2] I remember sitting at the table with customers who projected an exotic persona onto me, and I would be thinking I am just Marcia Fisher, the social worker!

My inspiration for dancing was a dancer named Amina. Although she was a very quiet, unassuming woman, married with children, she was a powerhouse on the stage. If she could do it, so could I. My experience as a professional dancer was one of pretending I was someone I wasn't, enhanced by the use of costumes and make-up. I would receive a great amount of attention when I was the belly dancer. Some of the other dancers began wearing their make-up and exotic clothes on an every-day basis and referred to themselves by their stage names. I never did! Out in the world I could blend into the background, and no one would notice me. That was my comfort zone.

What drew me to belly dancing? It was a love of movement and rhythm, and a love of the dance. I had been a dancer since I was very young. Tap dancing led to modern dance, which led to folk dancing, which led to belly dancing. Having been a wallflower and an egghead most of my life, I liked the attention people gave me when I danced. I did not fade into the background. I was no longer a victim, but now I had

---

[2] This practice is illegal, and women who did this were called B-girls, in other words, bar girls.

power. The power I am referring to comes out of sensual enticement and manipulation, and it is a form of witchcraft. Do you remember the Bible story of Herodias' daughter? John the Baptist was killed because she enticed Herod through her dance to give her anything she asked. And she asked for the head of John the Baptist! She manipulated Herod, and behind the scenes her mother manipulated her.

I performed at a club in Berkeley called The Babylon. In the back hallway above the pay phone someone had written a bit of poetry and attached it to the wall. I recall taking that fragment of paper and keeping it, as it spoke to me in some way and stirred my emotions.

> **By the rivers of Babylon, there we sat down, yea, we wept, when we remembered Zion. We hanged our harps upon the willows in the midst thereof. For there they that carried us away captive required of us a song; and they that wasted us required of us mirth, saying, Sing us one of the songs of Zion.**

It wasn't until years later after I had become a Christian that I recognized this as a quote from Psalms 137:1-3.

During this time I became friends with another dancer whose name was Linda. Jim and I spent a lot of time with Linda and her husband getting high and tripping on LSD. One weekend we went to the Russian River and took some mescaline. Jim had taken the same drug a couple of days before, and he thought it was great. I believe that I took a lesser amount than the others, however, I had a very bad trip. I totally lost contact with visual reality, meaning that all I could see with my eyes open was a greenish black color. I was having a very bad time, and they tried to give me another drug that was supposed to bring me down, but I vomited it up.

I remember the men being very concerned. I could hear their voices although I could not see them. They were considering taking me to an emergency room to get help, but we would all get arrested if they did that. I remember sitting on the bathroom floor of this motel so dizzy and nauseous that I could not stand up. My vision was beginning to return. Linda, who was sitting on the floor with me applying a cold compress to my head, said to me in a very matter-of-fact way, "Snap out of it, Marcia, or we will all get busted." She was not excited or full of anxiety as the men were, and it was her very calm and truthful statement of fact that sobered me up. I was grateful for her wisdom. For many months following that experience I had imprinted in my brain a connection between becoming high and severe nausea and dizziness.

Linda and her husband had an open relationship, and she had many extramarital affairs, often with her husband's knowledge. What I did not know was that she had begun an affair with Jim behind my back.

I had switched birth control methods after my pregnancy, but for some reason my doctor put me on the Pill for just one month. During that month I had a return of the severe intestinal cramping that had dominated my life for so many years. But this time I knew what was causing it: hormones! And all the time I thought something was wrong with me. Every time I got into a serious love relationship I would get sick. I had made the symptom psychosomatic when all along it was a side effect of a medication.

In 1972, Jim and I decided we wanted to go to India. It was mostly his idea, but I was adventuresome and said, "Let's go!" We sold our belongings, quit our jobs, and took a flight to Europe. We did the hippy thing and flew into Luxemburg and purchased a car in the airport. It was a cheap Volkswagen Bug, and it was cheap for a reason. The previous owners were trying to sell it before flying back home and gave us a good deal. It had several problems that would unfold as we began our travels. We had car trouble in almost every country where we traveled.

Upon arrival in Europe, Jim no longer had his regular fix of speed, and he crashed, wanting to sleep for days. I was withdrawing from marijuana and I was wide-awake. It was such a dark and lonely time. He was also depressed because of the separation from Linda, but I still did not know of their sexual relationship.

First we went to France and Spain, and then continued south to Morocco. It had been a long time dream of mine to visit Morocco. After taking the boat across the straits of Gibraltar, the Moroccans refused to let us enter their country. They would not give us a reason, but we believed it was because of Jim's long hair. We were clean and neatly groomed, drove a car, but they said no. We were both so disappointed.

We headed back up North. By this time Jim was very irritable because he had left all his drugs at home. Somehow he scored a brick of hashish and hid it under the car. Subsequently we crossed the border into France, Italy, Yugoslavia, Greece and Turkey with drugs hidden in the car. It added some daily anxiety onto the apprehension I already had about the trip.

One experience in Istanbul stands out. We had been out late at a nightclub that featured belly dancers, and for some strange reason the show started around midnight or later. We got back to our hotel that was in the center of the city, and at around 3 a.m. this plaintive sound could be heard. The muezzin were calling the prayers from the minarets at various parts of the city. The streets in Istanbul were quiet, which in itself was unique. You could hear the prayer being called from one minaret, and then another would echo back; it went on for several minutes. I was spellbound and transported into another state of consciousness. I felt at peace. There is such a phenomena as false peace that is not true peace. This type of peace is hypnotic. It is not the real peace of God where you can come into that place of rest knowing that He has everything under control.

We were on the road again and the traffic in Turkey was practically nonexistent. There were no people except for an occasional shepherd. Then we stopped in a small village for a tea break. On the streets and in the tea shop there was not a single woman present. The men certainly stared at me, a western woman who was in their midst. Some of the places where we ate were so primitive that I had to shut my eyes in order to eat what was put before me. I'm sure that I ate camel and goat, but the lack of hygiene was more of my concern.

As I previous mentioned, the car was consistently breaking down, and we had one of those occurrences in the mountains of Turkey. We had been warned that there were treacherous thieves in the mountains and that we needed to be careful, but when you can't start your car there is not a lot you can do. Several men appeared out of nowhere, and all of them wanted to get into the act of fixing the car. No one had any mechanical ability, and they did not speak English, but between Jim and them, the car finally started. They were so nice to us and genuinely concerned. They warned us though, about the fearful bandits in the mountains of Iran. They were cutthroat and would rob and hurt us, I suppose, like the ones we had just met.

The Turkish countryside was very beautiful and pastoral. I remember seeing Mt. Ararat rising out of the valley to the left as we headed toward Iran. The road leading up to the border station between Turkey and Iran was steep and full of hairpin turns. It was so amazing to me that there was absolutely no traffic! Inside the station hung a large picture, in a prominent position, of the Shah of Iran. His picture was displayed in all the public buildings. When we left the border the sun was starting to set, and I saw my first camel on the loose, roaming around. I jumped out and snapped a picture.

We stayed in Tabriz for a few days. It is a fairly large city with a very large souk, or market. Jim was feeling ill and took to his bed. My choices were to stay in the hotel and be bored or venture out by myself. I chose the latter. I had not walked far from the hotel when a young boy approached me and asked if I would go with him to see his brother's rug shop. I told him that I was not interested, but he was very persistent so I asked him if he would take me to find jewelry. We struck up a compromise; he would take me to find jewelry if I would first go to his brother's shop.

So off we went, entering into the souk's main tunnel, which was without natural light, although the shops kept it well lit. I believe our malls of today are fashioned after these Middle Eastern covered markets, but this market was larger than any mall I have ever been in. It was like a little town with shops lining the streets. On any given street the same type of goods were marketed, for example, one street would feature clothes, then you would turn a corner and go down another street where they sold pots and pans. My companion certainly knew his way around, and after a very long walk we entered the street where they sold rugs. By this time I was totally lost and dependent on my young friend to get me back out into daylight.

Each shop was quite small with the rugs piled up in the corner. I had told my guide that I really was not interested in buying rugs, that I had no space in my backpack for a rug, nor could I afford one. I said the same to his older brother. Nevertheless, they told me to sit, and they prepared tea for me served on a bronze platter. Then he began showing me every rug in the shop, describing the history behind each one. He asked me what I liked, and I responded that I liked older tribal pieces. I consented to buy a woven rug piece about twenty-four by fourteen inches that would fit into my backpack. I will never forget the wonderful hospitality bestowed on me. Then we went in search of jewelry, one street with gold and another with silver.

After I left the market I was walking back to the hotel by myself when two women wearing black shawls covering their heads approached me. They spoke to me in English and just wanted to talk with a Western woman. I had a similar experience in Afghanistan, and I will tell you about it later.

When it was time to leave Tabriz, a Persian young man approached us and asked for a ride to Teheran. We decided on the spot to take him with us thinking it would be wise to have someone who could speak Farsi accompanying us should something else happen to the car. This was the beginning of our friendship with Mahmud.

And sure enough the car broke down once again. We decided to have a picnic in a field while we waited for another car to come along. It was a long wait until finally a small truck stopped, and the driver came to our aid. He took a rope and tied our car to the back of his truck.   This was another of those traumatic experiences where I was very frightened. His vehicle was larger than ours, and I had visions of him stopping suddenly, our car crashing into his, and the three of us going under the bed of the truck, having our heads cut off. So I scrunched down as low as I could to the floor and closed my eyes in terror, but fortunately we made it to a mechanic's shop safely. Thankfully, he had the part and could fix the problem, so we proceeded on our way to Teheran.

Our friend took us to a hotel where he knew the proprietor and negotiated for us to sleep on the roof. This was inexpensive and very pleasant, as we had very comfortable beds on the roof. It was beautiful seeing the lights of the city at night and the stars. Mahmud also took us to small restaurants where only Persians frequented and ordered our food for us. I had been having intestinal problems since we left Spain; so I was eating lots of yogurt and chicken soup. We didn't mind at all paying for our companion's food and lodging and providing his transportation because he was such a help to us. He was also a delightful young man, and we very much enjoyed his company. Mahmud was really fascinated by Western women, Europeans and Americans, because he loved their independence. He made a regular habit of traveling with foreign tourists and offering his services as a guide.

I have more recently read about the role of Muslim women and how they are confined to their homes. That is why the streets are often devoid of women. They are essentially owned by their fathers first, and then by their husbands. They are not even allowed to stand near a window because no one is allowed to see them outside of the family. Any woman who is seen outside with her face and body not covered in the veiled outer covering is assumed to be a whore.[3]

Mahmud, a Muslim young man, actually enjoyed the willfulness and the independence of Western

---

[3] *Women Under Islam* by John Laffin, published by Jubilee Resources, 1997, p. 25.

women. He was always a perfect gentleman with me and respectful in every way.

I remember the three of us walking down the street together. I was walking behind the two men, and some of the other Persian men in the street would purposefully bump into me rather forcefully. This rudeness and rough behavior is explained when you understand their attitude toward women. I did not like their attitude one bit.

Mahmud helped us out of another potentially dangerous situation when we visited this special mountain in Teheran. We were climbing up a rather steep trail along which were picturesque cafes and teahouses. Somewhere on the trail we all became separated and a policeman accosted Jim. Fortunately, our friend intervened and got the policeman, who was threatening to arrest us if we didn't give him money, to retreat and leave us alone.

We left our car in a garage and journeyed to Isfahan south of Teheran by public bus. We thought it wise not to take any chances with the car breaking down again. The buses were made by Mercedes Benz and were very comfortable. Persian music was played throughout.

I have flown to other countries, and that is one kind of experience, leaving one culture and entering another. This trip by car was totally different. We were literally driving to the other side of the earth. I did not keep a record of the number of miles, but I had such a deep sense in my heart of getting further and further away from home. We would stop for tea in the afternoon and be the only people in the teashop besides the owner. The floor would be dirt and it was hot and dusty. The owner would put down his prayer rug and bow down toward Mecca. I would be filled with such a loneliness and sense of being lost and so far from home.

The last scary incident in Iran occurred as we were leaving by car. We parted from Mahmud in Teheran and headed east. We were on the highway, a two-lane road, when we came upon a small avalanche of rocks. The cars were backed up for a distance and everyone was afraid to proceed. But we were the brave and impatient Americans, so we moved out of the line and drove quickly past the place where the rocks were falling, and praise God no rocks hit us. The people cheered as we made it safe to the other side.

The border between Iran and Afghanistan was one of the most God forsaken places I have ever been. Inside the border station everything was gray and colorless. We gave them our passports to stamp in one room and then went into the medical clinic to show them our records of immunizations. All the rooms were devoid of decoration and had maybe a small wood table and one or two wood chairs for furniture. Everything was dirty and dusty. One definitely would hope not to need medical attention in such a place, and fortunately we were let through. We may have had hashish still hidden in the car at this time, although I don't remember.

The next stop was Herat, Afghanistan. Compared to Teheran this city was as different as night and day. Afghanistan was very poor and primitive in comparison. This was in 1972, and Afghanistan was still open to tourists. We found a very cheap hotel in the section of town for Westerners. It cost a couple of dollars a night and was very Spartan. We also met a young man there who wanted to help us, but he was more out to serve himself than us.

I was attempting to stay healthy, but I had been having gastrointestinal problems since we left Europe, and as I said before, I ate a lot of chicken soup and yogurt. It did not help! Rather than drink the local water in Afghanistan, we drank bottled orange soda, Coca Cola, and local tea. The soft drinks had different amounts in each bottle, and some were definitely short changed. This caused me to question their purity.

One day we took a horse and buggy ride into the older section of town. I had never seen such poverty in my whole life. The streets were crammed with people and animals in contrast to the western side of town where there were wide spaces with no people except an occasional tourist. I remember an old man there who was wearing a coat made from small scraps of cloth sewn together. It made a lasting impression on me. Now I think of Joseph and his coat of many colors or of some rich hippy that would have paid a fortune for that coat! However, it was for me an example of extreme destitution, and my soul ached for the plight of these people. Disabled children with deformities would crawl or scoot along the sidewalks begging for money. Poverty was everywhere.

Some local musicians came by the hotel every day and played music for small donations. I remember being fascinated by this unusual man. The whole time he was playing his instrument, a fly was crawling over his face, his mouth, and his nose; never once did he flinch, blow, or brush the fly away.

It was also in Herat that I was out walking in the street by myself when I heard this female voice speak to me in English. I turned, and there was a woman covered with the traditional covering of the burka. You couldn't see any part of her body except her feet. It was thrilling for both of us to be able to communicate. It was a minute or two of time but so special.

With all the car problems, we finally came to the conclusion it would be so much easier to travel by public transportation. We wanted to unload ourselves of excess baggage and also to sell our car. The first was easier, and we gave clothes to some of the local young men. I remember the smiles on their faces as they tried on our bright red plastic rain capes. What a gift!

Disposing of the car was more difficult. The car had been stamped in Jim's passport as a custom item, and it was illegal to leave the country without it. There were two young men that we had met who wanted to purchase the car, but in order to sell it, we had to travel to Kabul, the capitol, and bribe, or should I say give gifts, to some officials to get the car taken out of Jim's passport. So the four of us set out for Kabul. From Herat to Kabul it is a straight shot east, but in the middle are high mountains. Therefore, the highway goes south to Kandahar and then north to Kabul. The road was fairly new at that time and again, no traffic at all. On the last leg of the trip, we began having problems with the car. I could see sparks of fire through the hole in the floorboard. I remember that I started shaking uncontrollably with fear. Jim and I were not getting along too well at this point, and he was angry at my reaction.

We limped into Ghesnee and found a place to stay. The sanitary conditions in this town were deplorable.   But we were able to purchase a new generator for the car and be on our way. In Kabul, Jim was able to go to the customs office and, with some money put into the correct hands, he was able to have the car removed from his passport. So we were not sad to see our two Afghani friends drive off to Herat in that green Volkswagen.

In Kabul I became even more ill. I had lost considerable weight, and one day I passed what seemed to be a large amount of blood into the toilet. Jim, who had been a nurse, thought I probably had an ulcer. We were both scared because we knew this was no place to need medical attention. We decided that I should fly back to California, so out came the credit card, and I bought a one-way ticket from Kabul to San Francisco. The trip took over twenty-four hours with stops in Beirut, London, and New York, but finally I was home.

Chapter Eight

Following the Guru

Linda and her husband met me at the airport, and I stayed with them in their home. I did not have medical insurance so I had some medical tests through the health department, and everything came back negative. For weeks I had had severe pain in my intestinal tract, and after passing all the blood, I thought at least there should have been parasites. I weighed 106 pounds, the lowest I had weighed since my early teens.

I had no money and no job, and I did not know when Jim would return. I was eager to become self sufficient so I accepted a dancing job in Montana. While I was there, Jim returned to the U.S. He drove his car back from the East Coast, and it broke down outside of Reno. Linda went to pick him up alone. When I learned of this I became hysterical, for by now I knew of their relationship. How could her husband have allowed her to go and rescue him?

Linda left her husband, and she and Jim came to Montana to meet me. There began several weeks of hell on earth. I was so distraught that I could not sleep, so I consulted a doctor who gave me Quaaludes. I had never heard of the medication, and I did not know that people took them to get high. They made my extremities numb so I stopped taking them after about two nights.

Linda agreed to shoot speed with Jim; that was something I would not do. She used every feminine wile to get him to leave me and choose her. My relationship with Jim was based on a little more than sex and drugs, as we were friends. We could sit up all night just talking. But in the end this was not important.

When we returned to the San Francisco bay area I was abandoned, and the two of them went to live together. Linda rejected me, and she would have nothing to do with me, nor was I ever to step foot into their home. I was so traumatized by this experience that I was numb and in a daze. For example, I would put my purse in the refrigerator and then forget where I had left it. Jim would occasionally come by to see if I was O.K. My anger and hurt was more directed at Linda for her betrayal than at Jim, because I had learned some time ago that he could not be trusted.

Soon after this I went to a psychic masseuse who told me that I had no bitterness in my body from the experience with Jim and Linda. What a lie! It was years after my salvation before I could recognize that I had plenty of bitterness, but I had believed her.

I was still penniless and without a job, so I accepted another dancing job, this time at a nightclub in Vallejo, California. On the same bill were go-go dancers, a stripper, a comedian and myself, the belly dancer. At the nightclub I met another man who wanted to take care of me. Since I was destitute, I moved in with Bill. He was very good to me, and for the first time a man was taking care of me financially. I found it somewhat uncomfortable to receive his generosity.

That New Year's of 1973, the entertainers from the club were invited to participate in a New Year's Day show at San Quentin Prison, a maximum-security prison. I was not the least bit afraid although they gave us bodyguards every time we went to the restroom. Later I happened to catch myself dancing on TV during the evening news.

I needed more steady pay so I applied for a job again as a social worker in Children's Protective Services. I had said previously that I thought the most difficult social work job was investigating reports of child abuse and neglect, and making recommendations to the court as to whether a child should remain with their parents or not. Yes, wouldn't you know, that was the job I accepted. I wanted to be able to pay my own way. Bill said it was not necessary, but it was something I wanted to do to maintain my independence.

It was not too long before they made plans to close the plant where Bill worked. He put in for a transfer to Hawaii and asked me to come with him. At first I said no, but as the time got closer for him to leave, I changed my mind. By then he had changed his mind and did not want me to come. So he moved to Honolulu, and I was alone for the first time in several years.

I was so tormented; fear had taken over. I was afraid to be alone. This was foreign to me since I had been alone much of my life until the last few years. I knew that the fear was not who I was; it had overtaken my mind, but it was not me. My emotions were controlling me rather than me controlling my emotions. I was desperate to find some way to control this fear.

Someone had given me the book *The Master Game, Pathways to Higher* Consciousness by Robert S. de Ropp. This book talked about the varieties of yoga and meditation available to the Westerner. The only subject I remember from this book was the section on mantras. I had never heard of a mantra before. A mantra is a word or phrase that is repeated over and over in the mind, every waking moment. It is used to blank out the mind and open the door to "higher" consciousness. I was so desperate; I was not looking for higher consciousness, but I needed something to shut up my thoughts and emotions and give me peace. I began chanting the phrase: God help me, God help me, God help me, as in a mantra. I have later learned that chanting a mantra, even if it is a prayer or a quote from Scripture, opens the door to evil spirits.[4]

It was not long after that, that I began attending a meditation class. We were reading *Be Here Now* by Baba Ram Dass. The book did not make a whole lot of sense to me, but I do remember that it taught one how to find the right spiritual path and how to find a guru.

I have often been asked, what is a guru? The word guru means "from darkness to light," and a guru is a person who supposedly takes you "from darkness to light." This is right out of Hinduism. They say that the guru is greater than god because the guru shows you god.[5] Although I thought it was God with a big G, in actuality it was god with a little g. We are not to worship or bow down to any man; that is idolatry, which was punishable by death in the Old Testament.[6] However, I knew nothing about this at the time.

---

[4] I have learned much of what I know now about the dangers of occultism from Pastor Henry W. Wright and his ministry team. I learned that evil spirits take advantage of a passive mind.

[5] This is a quote from a speech given by Guru Maharaji.

[6] In Genesis 31:30-35 is the story of Jacob and his wife Rachel fleeing from her father, Laban. Jacob speaks a curse of death on the person who stole Laban's gods not knowing that his wife had done this. She later died during childbirth.

I was still working in Protective Services when I told a colleague about my meditation class and I invited her to attend. She said that she also attended a meditation class in San Francisco and invited me to come with her. I accepted her invitation and found myself at a meeting of Divine Light Mission, the organization of Guru Maharaji, the child guru who claimed to be god incarnate. I entered a room filled with people sitting on the floor and listening to a speaker. Everyone seemed so happy; they referred to it as being "blissed out." Never had I experienced anyone so high without being on drugs. I was attracted to these meetings because they made me feel so good. My experience with mind-altering drugs had made me sensitive to spiritual energy, and I was easily influenced by the energy around me. My mood would become more joyful when I was with the "premies."[7] So I began to attend the meetings regularly because it helped ease my depression and anxiety.

The guru gave a talk in which he said, "Come to me and I will give you peace. Give me your love and I will give you peace." There it was, what I was looking for, peace of mind. He also quoted from the Bible, and because I had never read the Bible, I was impressed. His favorite Scripture was:

... the kingdom of God is within you.
Luke 17:21

They taught a meditation where you learned techniques to turn inward, become passive, and focus on inner light, inner sound, an energy called "holy name,"[8] and an inner taste referred to as nectar. This

---

[7] This was the name for the devotees of Guru Maharaji. It means lovers of God and Guru Maharaji.

[8] Holy name was referring to the Word; however, they did not know that the Word is a person, Jesus in His preincarnate state, not an energy inside the body.

experience was named "knowledge of god." They said, "You don't have to give up your religion. This is not religion. This is 'knowledge of god,' higher than any religion." I learned later that this was a common lie told by other teachers of eastern meditation.[9]

Another favorite scripture that the guru used was:

If thy eye be single thy whole body will be filled with light. Matt 6:22 and Luke 11:34

They had used scripture out of context and interpreted it to justify their teaching. They taught us to meditate on the third eye, the 6th chakra, in the Hindu tradition. This opens you up to a spirit of divination giving you psychic experiences and knowledge of the future. Later, after becoming born again, I learned that I had opened my spirit to evil spirits who came in and took up residence when I had blanked out my thinking mind and had become passive, therefore turning inward to that kingdom within.

I never thought I knew anything about Hinduism because the guru said that he was not teaching Hinduism. That was not true; we were learning ancient techniques of meditation. In Hinduism, as in other new age modalities, the thinking mind becomes the enemy. The goal of the practice is to obliterate the mind; they would say it is to transcend the mind.[10] But I have

---

[9] I have heard this said of Buddhist meditation, and I have an article from the Columbus Ledger-Enquirer, 1-25-03, in which they quote a yoga teacher saying about yoga, "It's not Christian or unchristian. The true teachings are beyond name and form. Beyond Christ, beyond Buddha or Krishna."

[10] 1 Corinthians 2:16, " But we have the mind of Christ."

learned that God has given us a sound mind.[11] Why would we want to rid ourselves of it?

After about a month of attending meetings, I decided that I wanted to be initiated into this experience. My initiation took place in September of 1973. There the four meditation techniques were imparted. Everything about the meditation was to be kept secret. I did not experience much of anything during the initiation, but I was told to practice this meditation every day, and the experience would grow. I did this meditation for an hour every day for the next eighteen years of my life, seeking after mystical union with god. I had far out spiritual experiences, but had also opened the door to evil spirits.

My lifestyle changed. I stopped smoking cigarettes; I became vegetarian, although I did eat a little poultry and fish. I attended meetings almost every night. I moved into a communal living situation in Berkeley with other devotees. We had a large house, and seventeen of us lived there. I was probably the oldest since I was in my thirties. There were a couple of young people having their first experience living away from home. I remember teaching some of the guys how to use an iron and certainly how to cook.

My lifestyle became one of following the guru. In November 1973 he held a very large festival called Millenium '73 in the Houston Astrodome. This large new age event borrowed from Biblical prophecy, claiming that we were ushering in a thousand years of peace. This event, of course, never lived up to its title.

The guru had festivals literally around the world, and I went to many of the meetings, traveling to the East Coast, Canada, Spain, Italy and finally, to India and Nepal. The message was *satsang,* service and

---

[11] 2 Timothy 1:7

meditation. *Satsang* literally meant "the company of truth." We had meetings several times a week to share this experience with each other, in other words, to share the "truth." I also participated in volunteer work for the guru, especially in relation to the large festivals where I often volunteered to work in the kitchen preparing the food. I truly enjoyed working with large quantities of food; even in our little commune, I enjoyed cooking dinner for seventeen people, a skill I have since lost. Also I participated in large sewing projects, making beautiful gifts for the guru.

At the beginning of this experience my depression lifted. I foolishly thought I would never be depressed again. I think the enemy gives small rewards to keep one snared. I did have incredible experiences of my body being filled with white light, of becoming one with the energy of the universe, believing that this energy was God. Little did I know that there were evil spirits orchestrating my experiences and that I had contacted gods with a "little g" rather then the one true living God.

But there were also problems. I had become sensitive to synthetic fabrics. I noticed that I would have itching in my mouth when I wore certain clothes or when I sat on certain upholstery, and my allergies to pollens, mold and smoke had increased.

I had also become more open to other new age and occult activities. In the mid 70's I consulted an astrologer. This gentleman was very psychic, and he accurately predicted several events in my life. He told me the month that I would change jobs and would move into my own apartment. At that time I had no plans to do either, but it happened as he predicted it. I went to work for a hospital as a medical social worker. This suited my personality better because I believed that I was truly helping others.

I worked primarily in physical rehabilitation, but I also was referred to work with a woman who had lung cancer. This was my first experience getting close to anyone dying from cancer. It was an experience I will never forget. I was fascinated by the love poured out to her by her husband and two sons; I had never witnessed the expression of such love in a family. I also worked with a young man who died from leukemia. Coming out of these experiences I saw the need for a support group for cancer patients. There were two such groups in San Francisco, and after attending some meetings, I organized a support group for cancer patients in the East Bay.

This led me into more new age and occult modalities having to do with healing and also death and dying. Carl Simonton was a radiation oncologist who, with his wife Stephanie, put together a process of meditation and guided imagery[12] for cancer patients. I had read several testimonies of people getting healed using this technique, so I went to the Esalen Institute in Big Sur, overlooking the Pacific Ocean, to study with the Simontons. While there, I attended some meetings with Stanislav Grof, a pioneer in consciousness exploration, including the use of LSD for psychotherapy and working with dying patients.

I had read the books on death and dying by Elizabeth Kublar-Ross, and she was another of my mentors. Elizabeth's pioneering work led to the establishment of the hospice movement in this country. She became discredited when she reported having visitations by persons who had previously died. Towards the end of her life she suffered a disabling

---

[12] Visualization and guided imagery are an age-old occult technique of witchcraft and sorcery used to manifest something in physical reality.

stroke and became a very bitter person. I read an account in a local newspaper of her isolation in the southwest desert. I was able to locate her through contact with her family, and I sent her a letter testifying of my conversion and healing. I got no reply, but I am jumping ahead as I have yet to tell you about my disability.

One day in the mid 1980's I was doing my laundry at a laundromat in Berkeley when my eye caught an issue of Time Magazine that was open to the page on medicine. I could see the lead article, and two words stood out, death and bliss. I read an account of people who were declared dead for a few minutes and who had an experience of traveling through a tunnel into a place filled with light and music, often being met by someone who appeared as white light. This sounded like my experience while doing the guru's meditation. Both of these experiences were mystical experiences from the occult.[13] I tore the article out of the magazine and carried it around with me in my wallet for several years; I believed that it validated what the guru taught.

[13] Spiritual Counterfeits Project Journal, Near Death Experiences: Revelations from the Death plane, 1994.

Marcia riding an elephant at the Amber Palace
Jaipur, India 1981

Chapter Nine

More Occultism

Once you involve yourself with the world of the occult, one thing will lead to another, and that thing to another. It is amazing, and certainly the plan of an evil intelligence, to bring together synergistically different modalities of occultism. Through friends I had met at Synanon several years previously, I was introduced to Mind Dynamics. Mind Dynamics teaches a person occult methods of visualization and creative imagery in order to regulate one's brainwaves and to induce a meditative experience. From that meditative state we were taught how to heal ourselves and to materialize the experiences we wanted to have. This is a form of self-hypnosis and will open you up to evil spirits when you enter into the hypnotic state. Once you learn techniques like this you have no need for the Creator. You become your own god!

When Mind Dynamics shut down, some of the instructors went out on their own and founded E.S.T., Lifespring, and Actualizations. I also completed the E.S.T. training and Actualizations. Werner Erhard conceived of the Erhard Seminar Training known as E.S.T.,[14] and he was influenced by Mind Dynamics, Scientology, Zen Buddhism, Hinduism, and psychology, to name a few of his formative experiences. The training was a two-weekend experience designed to put

---

[14] The name E.S.T. was changed to The Forum. Currently Landmark Education owns and distributes The Landmark Forum.

you in touch with your human potential. The goal also was to achieve enlightenment, which was the realization that we are one with the universal energy. That universal energy is the pantheistic god of Hinduism and the New Age. All that sounds impressive, but what we are really talking about is an altered state of consciousness brought about by evil spirits. No matter how wonderful it may feel, it is still an experience of demonic possession. And it is not without its consequences.

In the E.S.T. Communications Workshop I had a revelatory experience. In one of the exercises we took partners, and we were supposed to read a certain passage given to us without any inflection of voice. At the same time we were supposed to communicate various emotions silently. My partner was a female psychologist, and we were quite successful in doing this. I was accurate in guessing which emotion she had been transmitting. At the end there was one emotion I could not discern. I became more and more anxious as I tried to figure it out. Finally it came to me that I had been getting it all along; it was fear. I had attributed it to my own anxiety. This experience was a big piece of the puzzle. In doing social work I would often feel angry or fearful for no apparent reason. I would own it and try to figure out what I was angry about or what I was afraid of. But in reality I had picked up from my clients their unspoken emotional state. In E.S.T. they were teaching us to become psychic, but I already knew how; I just was not aware of it.

Around 1980 I had a very frightening experience of disassociation. I woke up one morning and felt totally disconnected from my surroundings. I looked around my apartment and nothing looked familiar. I didn't know what I was supposed to do, what I should wear, where I was supposed to go. Coming from my experience with cancer patients, I believed that I had a brain tumor. I could not think of anything else that would explain what was happening to me.

A year or two previously I had changed jobs, and I was now working in a large medical center in San Francisco as an oncology social worker. I went to one of the neurologists whom I knew and asked to be examined. She ordered a CT scan of my brain and an EEG, both of which came back normal. She told me that I was depressed. I said, "No, I am not. I am anxious because I am having these experiences." So I continued to function in spite of this. Sometimes when I would be driving home from work I would forget how to get from my present location to where I wanted to go. This experience of confusion was very different for me, as I have always had an excellent sense of direction.

I happened to be browsing in a new age bookstore on Telegraph Avenue in Berkeley when I opened an astrology book about the transits of various planets. I knew enough about my own personal chart to know that I was under the influence of a Neptune transit. I was astonished to read an exact description of what I had been experiencing. It spoke of the confusion and the fog in the brain and feelings of being removed from reality. I had a rebellious thought that doctors do not have the answer, but astrologers do. That began a quest for me to find a good astrology teacher.

I recall being impressed with the intelligence of the astrologers I had met. They had to master, not only astrology, but also mathematics, mythology, literature and history. I began to take classes. I accumulated over one hundred fifty astrology books, and I began to do charts for all my friends. I wouldn't become friends with someone unless I first did their chart to discover my compatibility with them. I attended many astrology conferences, and my knowledge and ability grew. My favorite author and teacher was a woman who, in addition to being an astrologer, was a Jungian analyst. Astrology and Carl Jung go very well together because he was interested in the occult, and his sister was an astrologer. In the end my local astrology teacher committed suicide after suffering from AIDS.

In the early 1980's I took my vacation time and signed up for a tour of India and Nepal. The timing was coordinated with a spring festival with the guru in India. This was not a typical tour where you stayed in the best hotels and flew from place to place. The director, who was a woman, negotiated the ground transportation for the tour on a daily basis. We flew to Katmandu and from there traveled by local bus to other destinations in Nepal. The buses were gaily and ornately decorated on the outside. Inside it was colorless, and we sat on metal benches and held on to the seat in front of us as we bounced over the primitive roads in Nepal.

The entire experience was one of intensity: the humanity, the animals, the dirt and dust, the wind, the beggars, etc. I discovered that I could not be out on the streets but for a short period of time. Then I would have to retreat to my hotel room to meditate and recuperate. There exists such a thing as false peace. The guru's meditation gave me that peace, but I was not able to handle any stress without losing my peace. I was weak in my spirit rather than strong and had to do more meditation to get my peace back.

Once we crossed over into India we rode in taxis to our next stop. I remember our taxi going down a narrow road at a speed too fast for my taste. There were people, carts, bicycles, and animals walking on both sides of the road. It began to rain, and the windshield wipers did not work. This was very common in India. Mud was accumulating on the windshield. The driver would reach out the window with his left hand

and move the wipers every now and then so that he could see, all the while driving too fast. To make matters worse, it was growing dark. During this trip, which took several hours, I was sitting scrunched in with two others in the back seat with my eyes closed praying to be allowed to live.

Varanasi, formerly known as Benares, was our first destination. This is the holy city in India where it is considered the highest spiritual blessing for Hindus to be buried in the Ganges River. The funeral pyres where they cremate the bodies are right next to the water so that they can dump the ashes into the river. I remember wading in the Ganges, as I wanted to at least get my feet wet. In actuality this river is very polluted by Western standards. They say that the water moves fast enough to purify it, but occasionally there are dead bodies floating down the river. We also visited Sarnath where Buddha gave his first sermon. I purchased a small statue of Buddha there as a souvenir.

I had made arrangements to leave the tour for a few days to attend a festival with the guru, and I was to be met in the airport by someone from his organization. I had no idea who was meeting me or how they would be able to locate me. After waiting a period of time I found a telephone and called the number I had. It is very difficult to hear and be heard on long distance calls in India so I was yelling into the phone. My two escorts heard this woman yelling in English from across the airport, and that is how they recognized me.

We drove to the festival site, and all along the road people were walking with their belongings on their heads while they made their way to the festival grounds. They had been walking for days, some for weeks. The festival was held outdoors and the people stayed in tents. It was a large tent city where they had a special section for the westerners. We had our own cooks to make sure that the food was healthy and not too spicy for our palate. I stayed in a tent room with one other person. There were rugs on the floor, and we had twin beds with brand new quilts covering the beds. This was one of the best accommodations that I had in India. During the programs we had seats to the side of the stage up front. The westerners were well taken care of. Close to 100,000 people were in attendance.

One of the group celebrations at the festival was Holi. I had always believed that this celebration was one of the guru's special holidays, and it was a favorite of mine. At Holi the guru sprays everyone with colored water; in other words, he paints his devotees beautiful colors. After this festival I saw people in the streets all over India still wearing their guru painted clothes. Years later I learned that this is a Hindu festival in India, but the guru had told us that he was not teaching us Hinduism.

I had thought that if I had any health issues during this trip it would have been with my gastrointestinal tract, but I was incorrect. I was having problems with my respiratory tract. I had caught a cold from being out in the wind one of the first days that I was in Nepal. At the end of this festival I got caught in a sand storm and developed bronchitis. The place to get medical advice was at the local pharmacy. The pharmacist was well educated; you told him your symptoms, and he would prescribe the medication. I took a course of antibiotics.

It was a dry and windy time, and there was always dust and dirt in the air. That explained why everything was dirty in India. I rejoined the tour for the rest of the trip; we visited Jaipur and I rode an elephant and had my picture taken. After I returned to California, I had another experience of disassociation.

But this time I attributed it to the culture shock of returning home, and it did not last too many days.

Then I attended a massage school in Berkeley where I was taught how to become psychic with my hands; that is, we were encouraged to become very sensitive to energy fields in a person's body using our hands. I became a good masseuse; my only problem was that I picked up other people's symptoms. They would feel better, and I would feel worse. I psychically picked up the energy of the other person. I learned and experienced many different forms of massage that came from the occult. I later learned a quick rule of thumb in this area. If the massage form works with invisible energy rather than muscles, then it is of the occult.

At this time I also passed a state examination and became a licensed clinical social worker. I sailed through the written part of the exam with no problem but failed the oral the first time around. The owner of the massage school encouraged me and helped me see that positive excitement was on the same continuum as fear. I was able to become excited about taking the test and to transcend my fear of failing. I passed the oral exam this time. I gave up my license seventeen years later when I knew that I wanted to minister deliverance and healing in order to give back what I had been given by the Lord. But I am getting ahead of myself again.

Progressively, I was becoming sensitive to more things in my environment. However, I did not have a doctor who would believe that my symptoms were coming from the source that I had identified. So I stopped going to doctors. One day I read in a women's magazine about Environmental Illness, and I recognized I had that problem. They gave the name of a medical organization where I could find a doctor in my area who treated this strange modern-day illness.

So I consulted a clinical ecologist. Hearing her speak of her own experience was very frightening. She told me to get rid of all chemicals in my home, everything from cleaning supplies to finger nail polish. I tried to do as she recommended, but instead of my health improving, I grew more sensitive.

I then became acquainted with Stephen and Ondrea Levine through my work with Elizabeth Kublar-Ross. They were part of a project called The Dying Project. They taught conferences on death and dying from a Buddhist perspective. Because of my work with cancer patients and because of my own illness, I became interested in their work and developed a personal relationship with them. Stephen taught that we should make friends with death and should wake up in the morning and say, "This is a wonderful day to die." I remember chanting this as I drove to work.

I learned later that persons with chronic Environmental Illness usually have a spirit of death attached to them. I had certainly opened myself up to this spirit with all the studies I completed with Elizabeth Kublar-Ross and the Levines. A spirit of death can also come on a person when one asks God to let them die because they don't want to suffer anymore. Satan will come along to make that happen for you; only it doesn't happen quickly. He brings infirmity along with a spirit of death to fulfill your desire. The good news is that you can repent for this and cancel the devil's assignment.

Through the influence of Stephen Levine, I became interested in Vipassana, a Buddhist meditation practiced in Sri Lanka. I attended a ten-day silent Vipassana retreat in the California desert. Everything we did was a meditation: eating, walking, and sitting in silence. These experiences have a profound affect on one's brain. The goal was to not attach to one's thoughts but to let them float by. Again, the thinking mind is considered to be the problem.

In Buddhism, all suffering comes from attachments, that is, anything that one cares about, or has expectations of, or hopes for. The goal is to be without desire and to be totally in the moment. If I don't care one way or another, then nothing will move me or stir my emotions, and I won't suffer. This is antithetical to Christianity. Scripture tells us that if we delight ourselves in the Lord he will give us the desires of our heart.[15] So we are encouraged to have desires, to set goals; this is something I learned much later. Scripture also tells us that the Lord wept,[16] so obviously, he cared deeply.

I was attending a Stephen Levine conference on death and dying at a Catholic convent in Santa Rosa when I was having excruciating abdominal pains. My intestines felt like they were on fire, and I was becoming discouraged and hopeless. The doctors could not find anything wrong, but they called it irritable bowel syndrome, a catchall diagnosis when nothing shows up on an x-ray.

Someone at the conference recommended that I consult an acupuncturist in Berkeley whom they knew. That is how I first tried acupuncture. John treated me for about six weeks, and during that time he told me that he thought I had a food allergy. I don't remember why we thought it might be dairy, but that was the correct diagnosis. I gave up all dairy products, and the pain subsided. After this experience I became a fan of acupuncture. I was angry with the doctors who could not correctly diagnose my problem, and I felt rebellious.

---

[15] Psalm 37:4
[16] John 11:35

83

Thus began a long journey into alternative medicine. I gravitated to strange and far out treatments. I continued to see John, and I would go into his office and not say a word. He would check my pulses, look at my tongue, and tell me exactly how I was feeling. Was he psychic? I certainly never found any other acupuncturist who could do that.

I have found that once I delved into the occult, the experience grew. One thing leads to another, to another, etc., and before I knew it, my life was filled with occultism. At first there are successes that act as a snare, but down the road I was not healed, only made more sensitive. I believed that I must continue with my treatments in order to function. Now I was in both financial and spiritual bondage.

At one of the conferences I had attended, I met a gentleman who had undergone treatment for Hodgkin's disease. As soon as he was aware that I was a medical social worker who worked with cancer patients, he became very friendly with me. He wanted to know why there were no support services for those who survived cancer treatment. I had not thought about that before. If someone finishes the treatments - in his case, surgery, radiation and chemotherapy - and is declared free of cancer, that should be cause for celebration. What was the problem? He felt devastated by the treatment and was angry about his whole experience. In keeping with the poor choices that I usually made in relationships, we began dating and the relationship progressed.

After surviving cancer he was intent on discovering who he was as a human being and as a man. He had planned a motorcycle trip across the U.S. and back. We were planning to live together when he returned. We even discussed marriage. In my mind I thought this was the one. We talked on the phone and wrote to each other all summer while he fulfilled his dream.

I had recommended that he attend a Stephen Levine conference in another state on his way back. Something happened at that conference. To this day I do not understand what made him change. He did not come back; in fact, he stayed away. He broke off the relationship. When he returned he was angry and critical of me for my new age ideas and life style. It had never bothered him before. He retrieved his belongings that he had left with me for safekeeping, and that was the end of it. I truly lost control of my emotions. I was so angry. I felt used and abandoned; in truth that is what happened. Many years later, I had the revelation that people who have been abandoned, as he had been by a parent, will abandon others. It really was not so personal.[17]

---

[17] Pastor Henry W. Wright teaches that we should separate others from their sin; we do not have to become victims of another's sin. When we become a victim and suffer because of someone else's sin, we have bound ourselves to their sin and it becomes our sin.

Chapter Ten

Environmental Illness

My health had been marginal at best, and it further deteriorated after this traumatic breakup. I reduced my hours at the hospital. I entered therapy with a licensed psychotherapist who had trained at the Berkeley Psychic Institute and who taught drumming as a means of self-expression. In fact, I had contacted him about a drumming class. I thought I needed an outlet for my anger and pain, and I believed I could tolerate a drum from a standpoint of environmental sensitivity. He convinced me that I should try psychotherapy. Also he became one of my strongest allies as I progressively became more ill.

My healthy friends had pretty much abandoned me by now. They thought that my symptoms were exaggerated, and I was just trying to control them by saying I couldn't tolerate their cigarette smoke, or I couldn't go to one restaurant, but another was better for me. I remember declaring that I did not need anyone, that I could do this alone. I would show them! In spite of this vow of self-sufficiency, there was a man named David who was in and out of my life during these years. We had met several years earlier when I was living in the communal house with the guru followers. He was with his wife at the time, and later they divorced.

He began to pursue me, declaring his love for me. I thought he could not possibly love me, as he did not really know who I was. I allowed him into my life, although I frequently thought I had made a mistake.

In fact, my relationship with him paralleled the downhill progression of my disease process.

His ex-wife had become a born again Christian, and she did not want her young son to have anything to do with anyone who followed the guru. Since she knew I still followed the guru, she forbade David to take his son anywhere with me. This caused a problem since his son was number one in his life; he did everything for his son. One day we had a very unpleasant confrontation at her church when we were returning the boy to his mother. Joshua knew me and had visited at my apartment. His favorite topic of conversation was Jesus. That was all he would talk about. I did not understand why his mother thought I was so evil, and later I learned she was praying for my salvation. I know of no other person who prayed that I would find the Lord Jesus Christ.

In the meantime, my father, who had had mini strokes over the last several years, began to deteriorate further. He had a form of dementia caused by the strokes. I was not aware how bad it had become until my mother called me. She said that she had put my dad in a convalescent hospital, and he had fallen out of bed and had broken his hip. I was very upset that it had gone so far without my mother consulting with me. As a medical social worker I had helped many families make decisions regarding the care of their aged loved one.

I went home immediately since my father was undergoing surgery to pin his hip. The trauma of the surgery and the anesthetic resulted in the further deterioration of my father's mental capacities. My mother thought he couldn't live this way; he would die. My fear was that he would live many years in this confused state.

My mother, who was a strong person and who made all her own decisions, decided to put my father back in the same nursing home where he had his accident. I was very much opposed to this. This nursing home was the closest one to our house, and that was the main reason for my mother's decision. I visited all the major nursing homes in town and picked another one where I thought the care was superior, but my mother had made up her mind, and in the end I had to let go of it. He re-entered the home right before Father's Day. I had put up a banner in his room that said Happy Father's Day and had brought him a helium balloon. The decorations were stolen before the next morning, which helped to confirm my suspicions about this particular nursing home.

My father remained there for about a year and a half before he passed away. In the beginning of his stay, I went home every weekend to visit him. This took quite a toll on me physically and spiritually. He still recognized me when I visited and would greet me with "Hello, daughter." On one of the visits in April I had gone for a short walk. I remember it being quite windy that day, and I developed a respiratory virus that put me in bed for over three weeks. Every time I went outside and breathed the fresh air, I became worse, yet I did not make the connection between the air I breathed and my respiratory status. I finally realized what was happening, and that is when I began wearing a charcoal mask every time I went outside. From then on, I was afraid of breathing the outside air, and I was especially afraid of the wind.

My chiropractor said to me, "Are you going to die when your father dies?" This brought me up short and enabled me to see what had been happening. I had always felt close to my Dad, after all, my mother said I was just like him, and now I was going down hill as he was also. So I decided to pull back, and I stopped visiting so frequently. My father passed away in July of that year, six weeks before his eightieth birthday. His death was actually a relief for my mother and me, as it had been so painful to see him in this confused state. My mother and I grew closer after his death, as if he had been a barrier between us, and that barrier was now gone. I believe that she was jealous of his love for me.

The only contact I had with anyone with environmental illness was my doctor and the man who sold me air and water filters. I would call the latter and talk to him by phone because he was the only one who understood what I was going through. He gave me the names of a few others and recommended that I attend the monthly meeting for the environmentally ill. I contacted the people he recommended, and their stories frightened the bejabbers out of me. I was still functioning at work, but I had fear of becoming totally disabled and isolated because of my illness. It is Satan's plan to separate us from family and friends and to isolate us.

One day I received a newsletter from the Environmental Illness Association, and in it was an ad from a medical social worker volunteering to help people with their disability applications. I was not in need of this yet, but I contacted the author because I wanted to meet another medical social worker that had this illness. That is how I met Anita Louise Hill who has remained my friend until this day. Anita was, at the time, totally disabled with environmental sensitivities. She became my mentor, helping me negotiate the often complex world of the environmentally ill. I became her astrologer, and she did pendulum readings for me and taught me how to use the pendulum.

People with environmental illness have so much fear about what they can eat, what they can drink, and which supplements they can take. The fear is what motivates them to dip into occult knowledge to get the answer. The pendulum became our method of choice for accessing divination, knowledge of the future that comes from an occult source. If the pendulum revolved to the right, the answer was yes; and to the left, the answer was no.

I struggled to remain working. I had so much fear about becoming disabled and not being able to care for myself financially. The hospital had been laying people off to cut back on expenses. As I had seniority in my department, I was supposedly assured of a job; however, the rules changed as I became increasingly more disabled. Because they were remodeling various floors in the hospital, I would have to be accommodated as to where I could work and where my office could be located. So I was moved from one floor to another. One day I arrived to find my office door doused with perfume. They had to remove the door and replace it with another one to get rid of the smell. Who had done this? Was it on purpose to cause injury to me? I would never know the truth.

I had accepted the job of acting director of the department the last six months I was there. This was a challenge and a stressor in my life. I was driven to do a good job, all the while fighting against symptoms. I also wanted to hide my increasing limitations. Whenever I walked outside the hospital I would have to put on my mask. I would pass people who I worked closely with, and I would be invisible to them. Never did anyone acknowledge me as long as I had the mask on. My life was one of hurrying to get inside out of the wind, avoiding open windows, fresh air and drafts, and once inside, avoiding paint smells, cleaning smells, etc.

After they hired the permanent director, I took disability leave. I thought that I only needed to reduce the stress in my life, and my health would improve. Anita advised me to go out at least once a day to do something, an errand, whatever, in order not to become totally housebound. I did not improve and was forced to resign after another six months. My self-esteem plummeted when I was no longer able to be a contributing member of society. Little did I know that God loved me just as I was. I did not have to do anything to earn His love.

My medical diagnoses included: multiple chemical sensitivities also known as MCS/EI, hypothyroidism, candida colonization hypersensitivity syndrome, chronic viral myalgic encephalomyelitis, chronic intestinal protozoan parasitosis, chronic fatigue immune deficiency-dysregulation syndrome, tendonitis, multiple allergies/universal reactor, hypersensitivity urethritis, autoimmune endocrinopathy, electro-magnetic frequency sensitivity, asthma, chronic back pain/degenerative disc disease, depression, and diffuse fibromyalgia syndrome.

My sensitivity to fabrics was an area that caused me much distress. I could not find clothes that I could tolerate. It was either the fabric, the dyes or finishes that caused me trouble, I never knew which. The symptoms affected my brain. I would become dizzy, nauseous, and unable to think, talk and remember. I always attributed these symptoms to exposure to chemicals.

I was also allergic to foods, with symptoms that ranged from hives to asthma and intestinal distress. I had become a universal reactor. I rotated my foods, cooked only in stainless steel, used filtered water in cooking, and bought organic food as much as possible. With this regimen I could find enough to eat although my weight was somewhat low. I discovered that if I avoided certain foods for about two years, I could tolerate them again, just in time to eliminate what I had been currently eating, because now I was allergic to those foods.

My friendships were with others who had this disease, with the exception of David who would disappear for months at a time only to reappear again. For the most part, my social contacts were telephone contacts. Anita and I spoke with each other almost daily. This is how I met Bruce Gridley, over the telephone. He was another social worker who had this disease, and someone had recommended that he talk with me. Bruce, Anita, and I have remained friends over the years and now serve the Lord together.

I had been living in the Berkeley hills for over ten years in a mother-in-law apartment when my landlord decided to sell his house. The new owner did not want someone with my problems living next to her, so I was given three weeks to move. I had no idea where to go. I did not know if I could tolerate living in a conventional apartment surrounded with healthy people who smoked, wore perfumes, cleaned with bleach, etc. Anita had advised me that the most important thing in finding an apartment was to find management who would be supportive of me. Three weeks was not a lot of time to look, but God was with me as I found an all-electric apartment where they did not use pesticide, and no one smoked on the floor where the vacant apartment was located. The manager was an elderly lady in her eighties. She took pity on me and promised that they would not rent to anyone who smoked on that floor or in the apartment below me.

I rented the apartment and started cleaning it thoroughly using my special cleaning supplies. I reacted every time I entered the apartment so I did not know if I could live there or not. Anita told me that it was possible to make almost any place livable with some aluminum foil and tape. It was 1988 when I moved in across the hall from the manager who became a dear friend. Daisy had other reasons for renting the apartment to me. Her husband had dementia, and she liked the idea that she had a medical social worker living across the hall from her. The first twenty-four hours in my new apartment were pretty scary, but as I relaxed I seemed to be all right. It was going to work for me.

One fall day in 1989, while I was having an appointment with my psychotherapist in Berkeley in his second floor office, everything began to shake violently. We looked at each other and both of us knew that it was an earthquake, a really bad one. I sat there holding on to my chair for dear life for what seemed to be a long time. After it subsided my therapist walked with me downstairs to my car, and on the way I happened to glance at a television, just in time to see part of the Bay Bridge collapse and a car go over the edge. That put terror into my heart.

I drove home slowly as all the traffic signals were out. My apartment was on the third floor, and I did not know what to expect when I opened the door. Everything was intact except for a potted plant that fell off a low table and spilled dirt on the floor. I had a small, delicate porcelain statue of a Sufi whirling dervish that sat high up on a shelf. It was upright and looked as if it had not moved an inch.

The electricity was off for approximately twenty-four hours. Bruce, Anita and I conferred with each other by phone making sure that we were O.K. Bruce had been outside loading his car. He said it was like trying to stand up in a roller coaster with the sidewalk going up and down. This had been the Loma Prieta earthquake, and it registered 6.9 on the Richter scale.

My communication with Anita was always by telephone. We got together once a year on Christmas Day. I would go over to San Francisco to her foil-lined apartment where we would eat the lovely dinner she had prepared. We usually started planning the menu in

September and dreamt about the food until December. Dinner would consist of foods that were our least allergic foods. Tofutti[18] was a special dessert for me, but Anita abstained.

We exchanged small gifts, and then for a yearly treat we would go to the movies. To my surprise many people in San Francisco attend movies on Christmas Day. Bruce came with us one year. What a sight we made: Bruce with his white, cotton gloves and respirator, Anita with her oxygen tank and syringes in her pocket should she go into anaphylaxis, and me with my respirator, oxygen tank and scarf around my head. It never ceased to amaze me how I could survive all these activities and not become any sicker. Actually, these Christmas days were some of my favorite times, and I added them to my bank of good memories to replace some of the older ones.

Other holidays were more difficult. I was usually housebound on the Fourth of July and Labor Day. Often it would be really warm. I would not open the windows because of my sensitivity to the air, and it could be ninety degrees indoors. The heat alone would make me ill. I had a big case of self-pity at these times, feeling sorry for myself because I was alone and not able to participate with the rest of the world. On Thanksgiving, I sometimes treated myself to a takeout dinner from the local macrobiotic restaurant.

As part of our networking with others with this illness, we would often hear of new treatments that someone had tried. There were few treatments that I could afford or tolerate. Anything considered experimental was not covered by insurance, and traditional doctors did not recognize this illness. Often the treatments would make me more sensitive. I did

---

[18] This is an ice cream substitute made from tofu.

transfer factor, IV gamma globulin, a milk fast to kill parasites, and sublingual desensitization drops - to name a few treatments prescribed by medical doctors. I bought medications available in Mexico or Switzerland that had not been approved here in the U.S.

I was driven to find a treatment that worked. In seeking out alternative treatments, I did homeopathy, chiropractic, acupuncture, radionics, herbology, medical hypnosis, reiki, and polarity therapy. I drank my own urine, which is a remedy from India. In addition I continued seeing my psychotherapist and a minister from the Unity Church. I also received psychic healings at the Berkeley Psychic Institute. And I would consult my astrological chart seeking knowledge of what the future held. In addition I studied yoga and tai chi. Anita and I both became radionics practitioners. A radionics machine[19] in those days cost approximately $1200. I have no recollection of how I got that much money together.

_____

[19] Today radionics machines cost approximately $3000. "Are you looking for a powerful, simple way of performing real magic and sorcery? Learn about amazing radionics machines that are like psychic energy amplifiers." www.radionicsmagic.com

Protesters Disrupt Allergy Conference

Patients say they're not being taken seriously

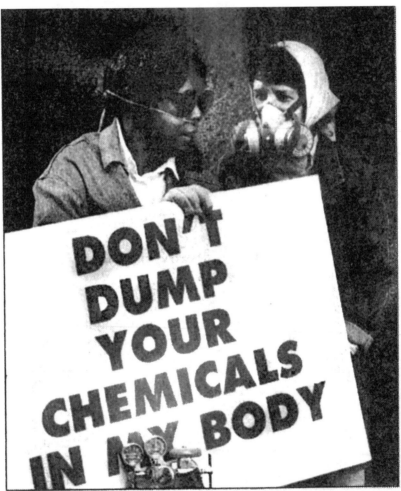

BY FREDERIC LARSON/THE CHRONICLE

Anita Hill (left) and an unidentified protester stood outside the San Francisco Hilton Hotel, where the scientific meeting took place

1990

Chapter Eleven

Disability

One day Anita called and told me of a vision she had. She saw the two of us walking at the beach, and we were totally healed! I wept. I could not even imagine myself walking outside without a mask, especially at the beach where it was foggy and windy. It had been so many years since I had been able to enjoy the out-of-doors.

I remember crying out to God telling him how my life was such a waste. I believed that I had no value as a human being. I had no family, no children, and I could not even work. I wanted to make a contribution, to make the world a better place to live. It didn't matter what I had accomplished before becoming disabled; none of it had much value. I felt stuck in this phase of my life, consumed with illness, disability, and self-pity.

In 1990, Bruce, Anita, and I picketed a convention of traditional allergists who did not recognize Multiple Chemical Sensitivities as a legitimate illness. Anita had many articles written about her, so the journalists recognized her and snapped our picture. So, there we were, Anita and I, with our picture in the San Francisco Chronicle. The caption read "Anita Hill and an unknown protestor." I was the unknown protestor. My mother always read the Chronicle over breakfast, so I telephoned her to ask if she had seen my picture in the paper. She had not recognized her own daughter because I was wearing my respirator and scarf, and Anita was on oxygen.

By this time I had graduated from a charcoal mask to an industrial respirator. The latter gave me more mobility, but even then I could not be outside for more than ten to fifteen minutes without becoming ill. My appearance at the allergy convention lasted only twenty minutes, and I was sick the entire next day.

When I was ill, I used to think about writing a book about my experiences of wearing a mask or respirator. I had people come up and in a hostile gesture offer me a cigarette. I had other people beat on the hood of my car and point their finger at me. Little children were always afraid of me and would hide behind their mothers. In general, people thought I was contagious. Little did they know that I was protecting myself from them! It was difficult to communicate through a mask, and I would have to raise my voice to be heard. The entire experience separated me from the rest of humanity. As mentioned previously, a common tactic of Satan is to isolate a person from fellowship, love, and emotional nurture. I had personal contact with so few people; that is why my practitioners and therapist became my allies.

One day as I was watching TV, I happened to see a Christian healer on one of the talk shows. She was having a healing service at the civic center in San Francisco, and I suggested to Anita that we try to go. So Anita, her roommate Dana, another friend, and I all went to listen to this woman. We had a long wait before it started, so we played a game that Dana had brought. Dana told Anita that she did not know what to do because she was Jewish. Anita, who was an ex-nun, said, "Just do what I do."

Towards the end of the service, the Christian healer began giving altar calls for various diseases. We all stood there waiting, wanting to go up, but nothing seemed to pertain to us. Finally, she said, "blood disorders." Well, we thought that was close enough, so we joined the long healing line. As she came down the row laying hands on everyone, people were falling down to the floor, but when she laid hands on us nothing happened; we were still standing. It was a miracle that I could even be in the auditorium for the six hours that we were there, even though I used oxygen and a mask. And Anita did have ringing in her ears to leave that night for a brief period. Later Jesus, through Pleasant Valley Church (now Be in Health™), did much better; He healed three out of the four of us. In fact, He healed all of us who came to Him.

I began watching the 700 Club on TV every morning. I looked forward to hearing the testimonies of healing. I prayed the sinner's prayer at the end of the program without having an understanding of what I was praying. I believe that seeds were sown that would later bear fruit.

My fiftieth birthday was approaching, and I was very depressed about the coming event. I was continuing to have problems finding clothes that I could tolerate, and I was down to just a few outfits. In fact, I had one blue denim jacket that I wore everywhere. I had to wear a scarf to cover my ears so that I would not get an earache when the air touched my ears, and I even had problems finding a cotton scarf I could tolerate. I was turning fifty and thought my life was over.

One thing I liked about my life was that I had done so many different things. I considered my experiences to be chapters in my life: the Italian chapter, the hippy chapter, the guru chapter, etc. Now I was afraid that I had become stuck in the "disabled" chapter, and this was the end. I remembered an astrology book I had read by Liz Green about cycles of time: a century, a year, a week, etc. The author said there had to be a dying off of the old before the new could be ushered in. So, I decided that I must be in the death throes of that fifty-year cycle, and ending the first half of my life before I started a new cycle called the second half of my life.

So I invited a few friends to come to my apartment for a small birthday party to celebrate the beginning of this new cycle. All went well except I had to ask one of my women guests to leave. There were skunks near where she lived, and she smelled just like them, and the smell gave me severe cerebral symptoms. This was how I ushered in the second half of my life!

Since I was not able to travel for some time, I had stopped going to meetings held by the guru, but I never gave up my daily meditation as taught by him. Instead, I began attending a local Unity Church, and because of my allergies, they allowed me to sit by myself in a small prayer room off of the main sanctuary where I could listen through a door opened a few inches. The pastor was a charismatic woman who would speak of Jesus one Sunday, and the next Sunday she would teach about Arjuna from Hindu scripture. So, the teaching was perfectly compatible with what the guru had taught. She became well known for her thesis on the Prayer of the Heart, and I briefly practiced the Prayer. This prayer was a mantra, even though she recommended repeating a Christian prayer.

A mantra is a powerful spiritual experience that I would not recommend to anyone. The goal is to quiet the emotions and thoughts, and in reality it is a technique of mind control. It actually opens the door to evil spirits who take you into an altered state of consciousness. It is also possible to have experiences brought to mind from the past that are very traumatic.

One Sunday I went to church and received a major shock. They announced that a female intruder had murdered the pastor earlier that morning. The intruder escaped in a car and was subsequently killed in an auto crash. It later came out that the murderer was someone who thought she heard Satan telling her to kill the pastor. I was traumatized! Everyone said that it affected me much more than the rest of the congregation.

Some months later I left this church and began attending a small congregation led by another female pastor in Lafayette in the East Bay. On Oct. 20, 1991, I had gone to church by way of Caldicott tunnel that goes through the hills from Oakland to Contra Costa County. When I came out of church, there was a huge cloud of smoke coming up from the hills. As I started to get onto the freeway, I saw that the cars were backed up so I made a quick decision to get off the freeway and backed down the on-ramp on the right shoulder. I had a tremendous fear of getting caught in a traffic jam, and I had fear of the smoke that was now quite black on the other side of the hill. I was so driven by fear I could have accomplished anything at that point. So now I had to drive around the bay the long way, and as I was coming back north toward Oakland, I could see huge clouds of black smoke. I still had no idea what the origin of this smoke was, but I was driving into it. Smoke had become one of my worst stressors, and I was terrified.

I finally arrived home, and I frantically ran around my apartment taping the windows and the sliding door shut to keep the smoke out. I even closed the curtains because it really frightened me to look out.

Cinders were flying through the air, and it was very dark. The bathroom was the only room without a window so I went in there with my air filter, oxygen tank and respirator, and called Anita on the telephone. She had the news on, so she told me the fire had started the previous day in the Oakland hills, and they thought they had it out, but the warm October wind had started it up again. It was a virtual firestorm now that had jumped the freeway and was destroying thousands of homes in its path. Anita told me to come over to her apartment in San Francisco, but since I could not tolerate her apartment for more than an hour or two, I did not think that was a viable solution. I decided I would have to take my chances at home.

By the next day the fire was contained, and I was elated that I had survived as well as I did. This fire destroyed 3000 homes, and the smoke from it was described as very toxic. Also it came within a block of my former apartment in the Berkeley hills. My health plummeted to even lower depths in the days and weeks following. I literally could not tolerate any of my clothes except for one old pair of jeans that had holes in the knee. And that was not a fashion statement! I had one cotton flannel shirt, and I wore this outfit for ten months. What caused me to lose my clothes was washing them. I was afraid to wash my clothes for fear of not being able to wear them again. My symptoms were dizziness, nausea, and inability to think and talk, so this was not something I could just ignore or rise above. I took a bath everyday, but I put on the same old dirty clothes. I know I must have smelled like a homeless street person.

I began experimenting by washing my clothes in different substances and keeping a journal as to the results. My landlord had allowed me to have my own personal washing machine in the laundry room, and I had put a two-stage water filter on this machine. I thought my reaction might have been caused by mold so I was trying different things that would kill mold. I washed clothes in the machine and also by hand using various substances such as baking soda, vinegar, hydrogen peroxide, sodium hexametaphosphate, etc. If I dried my clothes in the dryer, I couldn't tolerate them because they would smell like the electric dryer for at least a week, and by then they would be moldy again. If I dried them in the bathroom they would be moldy the next day. I even put my underwear in the microwave to kill the mold, and my bra caught fire. It's funny today, but it wasn't then! Nothing worked and this felt insane to me. In retrospect, I think I could say I had an unclean spirit.

I became so sensitive that I could not be around David at all. Previously, when he came to visit me he would take a shower the first thing and put on some of my old clothes, but now I couldn't tolerate even that. So I released him and told him not to feel any obligation toward me. He took this literally and disappeared out of my life after more than a ten year relationship. More rejection! But I was so into survival mode that I couldn't give it much attention.

I believe there are people who thrive on relationships with the weak and infirm, and when the sick person begins to change and become less dependent, the relationship is no longer satisfying for the healthy person. The sick person believes that no one else could possibly love them, and so they stay in a very unhealthy relationship. I had done this. I never heard from David again, although I know he heard from mutual friends that I was later healed. In fact, my automobile mechanic was far more excited about my healing than David. But I'm getting ahead of myself again.

It was late November when Anita called me and said that she had received a phone call from her former roommate, Dana Miller.   Dana had gone to the Christian healer with us, and now she had become a Christian and Jesus had healed her. I couldn't believe what I was hearing. Dana was Jewish, a feminist, and a New Ager. How could she have become saved? And God healed her! Incredible! I cried the rest of the afternoon. Anita did not understand why I was sad, and asked, "Aren't you happy for Dana?" Yes, I was, but my crying didn't have anything to do with that. I had been talking with God and I asked Him, "Is this what I have to do to become well?   Do I have to become a Christian?" You see, Christianity was far right of my leftist spiritual, political and social beliefs. I recognized it, as did most New Agers, as a legitimate pathway to God, but one that I had never considered exploring. I thought that all Christians were narrow minded, prejudiced individuals. I did not understand that their opinions were based on spiritual principles in the Bible rather than their own ideas.

I looked around my apartment at my altar with pictures of the guru, a statue of Buddha, and a Sufi statue. I had over one hundred fifty astrology books. I had a file box filled with astrological charts of my friends and others who had consulted with me. I had a radionics machine that I used to send healing vibrations to myself. I made all my own homeopathic remedies on the machine psychically intuiting the correct potency. I had many books on natural healing including psychic healing. I had many ethnic objects coming out of other religions that I purchased in my travels to foreign places. And somehow I knew that all of these things that were so much a part of my life, would have to go if I became a Christian. I said to myself, "Well, you think you are very spiritual. You have had these wonderful experiences of your body being filled with white light, becoming one with universal energy, hearing celestial music and so forth, but look at you! You're a mess! You are going to die if something does not change. You have so much knowledge, but you can't even heal yourself."

So I decided to lay it all down, and I grieved the loss of the person I thought I was. I later learned a Bible verse that described what I had to do.

For whosoever will save his life shall lose it: but whosoever will lose his life for my sake, the same shall save it.   Luke 9:24

Actually I was blessed to have hit rock bottom at that time in my life, otherwise I never would have considered giving up my life and looking to Jesus Christ.

Anita and I both contacted Henry Wright's church. These were the people who had ministered to Dana, and we began talking with them over the phone. In my first conversation with the woman who was to become my phone minister, she began talking to me about the Devil and his plan for our lives. It made perfect sense to me. For years I had been trying to get ahead, and every new treatment I tried, even though it helped others, did not help me. Often it would make me more sensitive, and I felt as if I were banging my head against the wall. I had even told my therapist and the Unity pastor that I felt as though an evil force was holding me down, but they both discounted this idea. When she told me about Satan, I said, "Yes, that is what was happening to me." So, after talking with her, I made a decision that I would lay down what I thought I knew and would see what she could teach me. If it did not work, then I could always go back and pick up where I had left off. I was told to get a King James Version of the Bible, and she would do Bible study with me. So I went to the Unity bookstore and bought the cheapest Bible I could find.

Marcia's 50th Birthday
1991

The medicine shelf

Chapter Twelve

Meeting the LORD

My phone minister, Nellie Lower, was an excellent Bible teacher. We talked by telephone for many months. She had me read the book of Luke first, because of all the stories of healing, and after that, the book of John to understand the Deity of Christ and also to become acquainted with the Father. She referred me to the Psalms: 103 for healing and forgiveness of sins, 104 for creation, 91 for fear, 139 for feelings of unworthiness, and Psalm 51 for repentance. (Refer to Appendix A)

I learned that God is not the universal energy of the New Age as I had previously thought, but He is a person. She encouraged me to develop a relationship with Him and to talk to Him just like I would talk to a friend. I also learned that God gave us free will to choose whom we would follow.

> **I call heaven and earth to record this day against you, that I have set before you life and death, blessing and cursing: therefore choose life, that both thou and thy seed may live: That thou mayest love the LORD thy God, and that thou mayest obey his voice, and that thou mayest cleave unto him: for he is thy life, and the length of thy days...**
> **Deuteronomy 30:19-20**

She recommended that I praise God through everything, including bad reactions. We read the story of Jehoshaphat and how the Spirit of the LORD came in the midst of the congregation. He fought their battle for them when they praised the LORD.

> Thus saith the LORD unto you, Be not afraid nor dismayed by reason of this great multitude; for the battle is not your's, but God's. 2 Chronicles 20:15

> . . . he appointed singers unto the LORD, and that should praise the beauty of holiness, as they went out before the army, and to say Praise the LORD, for his mercy endureth forever. And when they began to sing and to praise, the LORD set ambushments against the children (of the enemy) and they were smitten. 2 Chronicles 20:21-22

I was taught that the Old Testament presented a physical picture of our walk in the Spirit. Nellie told me to learn how to praise God as David did in the Bible.

She taught me the importance of the spoken word. Jesus was there from the beginning in his pre-incarnate state as the Word, and He spoke the world into existence.

> In the beginning was the Word, and the Word was with God, and the Word was God. The same was in the beginning with God. All things were made by him; and without him was not any thing made that was made. In him was life; and the life was the light of men. And the light shineth in darkness; and the darkness comprehended it not. John 1:1-5

> In the beginning God created the heaven and the earth. And the earth was without form, and void; and darkness was upon the face of the deep. And the Spirit of God moved upon the face of the waters. And God said, Let there be light: and there was light. Genesis 1:1-3

She read to me the story of Nicodemus and how Jesus told him that he must be born again. I was ready. I wanted Jesus to come into my heart. She led me to the Lord, inviting Jesus to be Lord over my life. We read Psalm 51 together. I repented and asked the Lord's forgiveness for my sins. I became born again before the end of my fiftieth year. I had truly begun the second half of my life!

I learned that if I had hope, I had faith. I could go boldly to God and ask for what I needed, providing I did not feel guilty, because guilt would separate me from God. I had felt guilty for some time believing that God was punishing me, but I learned that sickness is not from God; it is from the Devil.

How God anointed Jesus of Nazareth with the Holy Ghost and with power: who went about doing good, and healing all that were oppressed of the devil; for God was with him. Acts 10:38

Nellie taught me to speak to the mountain of fear and to the mountain of sickness, and command them to be removed.

And Jesus answering saith unto them, Have faith in God. For verily I say unto you, that whosoever shall say unto this mountain, Be thou removed, and be thou cast into the sea; and shall not doubt in his heart, but shall believe that those things which he saith shall come to pass; he shall have whatsoever he saith therefore I say unto you, What things soever ye desire, when ye pray, believe that ye receive them, and ye shall have them. Mark 11:22-24

Verse 25 says that in order for this to happen, you must forgive first. You can't have bitterness in your heart and expect God to answer your prayer.

And when ye stand praying, forgive, if ye have ought against any: that your Father also which is in heaven may forgive you your trespasses. But if ye do not forgive, neither will your Father which is in heaven forgive your trespasses. Mark 11:25-26

Speak to that mountain: Spirit of fear, you are not going to hold me in bondage because Jesus Christ sets me free. You are not going to stop me. I put fear under my feet. Satan, it is written:

For God has not given me a spirit of fear; but of power, and of love, and a sound mind.
2 Timothy 1:7

The enemy may not flee the first time you pray like this, but think of yourself as a teacher in the classroom. You have to have perseverance to get the children to be quiet. It takes practice to speak with authority.[20]

Then the day came when I was taught about the Baptism with the Holy Spirit. The Bible says that Baptism with the Holy Spirit is needed in order to do the works of Christ.[21] I was so excited because I never thought that I too could learn to do the works of Christ. Nellie prayed over the telephone that I would receive this baptism.[22]

I had always enjoyed African American gospel music. Anita and I both enjoyed Tramaine Hawkins, and we listened to several of her tapes. On Sunday mornings, since I could not go to church, I would listen to praise music on the radio. The soul music station was our favorite. What I liked most about the older gospel music was that the musicians praised God for what He had already done for them and for always being there for them in their time of need. I can count on you, God, to lift me up when I am down. It was a big faith builder.

Anita left at the beginning of the year to go to the southeast for her ministry of deliverance. Another

---

[20] Luke 10:19

[21] Acts 1:8, 4:31, 10:38, 1 Corinthians 12.

[22] The same ministry as is done in person can be done over the telephone. The only exceptions are Water Baptism and laying on of hands.

E.I. friend of mine also moved out of the area at this time, so I felt alone and abandoned. I read Scripture for solace, and I had this wonderful experience of discovering things that I grew up hearing my mother say. There was so much in the Bible that I recognized, but had no idea that Scripture was the origin.

Some of my reactions to the environment took the form of profound fatigue. This was not ordinary tiredness, but a fatigue so great that I could not sit up or stand, and I would have to lie down. I discovered that if I took my Bible to bed with me and read scripture out loud, especially the Psalms, that my energy would come back up to normal. There were other times when a reaction to my environment would produce excess energy. These reactions were less frequent, and I usually used the energy to do chores. But this was not normal energy either. I found at those times that if I read my Bible, my energy would come down to normal. This was quite a revelation for me. The Word was new and exciting in my life. I had hope that every word of God's promises to me was true and that He would heal me.

At that time, Bruce and I were attending a new age support group for people with serious health problems. This group was sponsored by the Center for Attitudinal Healing and was loosely based on the *Course in Miracles*. This course was dictated by a spirit guide who said he was Jesus to a Jewish psychologist. She gave herself over to this spirit and wrote down everything he said using a process called automatic handwriting. The course became popular through the books of psychiatrist Jerald Jampolsky.

I began telling people in our group to start reading the Bible, especially out loud. I think one or two of them did that. Scripture tells us that God's word will not return void.[23]

I knew only one Christian who had MCS/EI, and I spent a lot of time with her. Together we made Scripture signs for my apartment. I had a picture of clothes on a clothesline, and I wrote the following Scripture as a caption:

> **Wherefore, if God so clothe the grass of the field, which to day is, and tomorrow is cast into the oven, shall he not much more clothe you, O ye of little faith. Matthew 6:30**

One of the first things that God healed for me was my thyroid. I had been diagnosed hypothyroid for most of my life, and for the last several years I had taken medication. One day when I took my medication I noticed that I felt very hyperactive and nervous. It continued for a couple of days, and I discovered that I was taking too much medication. I gradually decreased the dose with my doctor's supervision and have not taken any thyroid medication since 1992. My thyroid blood tests are normal.

One day I was taking a bath and forgot that I had something cooking on the stove. When I came out of the bathroom there was a six-inch layer of smoke all around the ceiling of my apartment. I quickly opened the windows and left the apartment to sit in my car. I was so distraught. I stayed away for an hour or two then returned and phoned the church. The phone minister prayed against fear and stress and commanded my hypothalamus to bring my body chemistry into homeostasis. I was able to sleep in my apartment that night with the windows closed which

---

[23] Isaiah 55:11

was a small miracle! I never would have been able to do that without the prayer.[24]

Sometime in the spring, my neighbor a few houses down decided to put his printing business in a newly built structure in his back yard. That meant there was a printing press almost under my window. I questioned the legality of this because I lived in a residential neighborhood. There was the noise factor, but I was more concerned about the smell of ink making its way to my windows.

My landlord told me to write to the zoning department, so I wrote a letter, and a hearing was scheduled. Certain things began to happen. One day two tires on my car were slashed while the car was in a locked garage under the apartment building. Then someone doused my mailbox with perfume, and I had to throw out my mail for several days. I had my suspicions about who was doing this. Later I discovered that my letter was part of public record, and anyone would see that I had made the complaint.

I phoned the church and was telling them of this great injustice that had been done to me, and to my dismay the minister began praying against self-pity. I was somewhat offended. But I noticed later that afternoon that I felt really good. I connected how great I was doing to the self-pity issue, and I decided I did not care what she prayed for, as long as I got such good results. That experience was a lesson in discernment. I didn't really know when I was into self-pity, but I have learned that self-pity can make me feel totally miserable and the absolute worst. When I am

---

[24] The hypothalamus is the master gland that controls most aspects of daily life: sleeping, eating, temperature, sexual drive, etc. Its job is to keep the body in homeostasis by regulating the endocrine system. Pastor Henry Wright teaches about its functions in "Fear, Stress and Physiology."

having a really rough time and don't know why, I will take responsibility for self-pity, repent for it, and command it to leave in the name of Jesus. I then feel so much better.[25]

I had received news that Anita was healed, and she was walking out her deliverance. This gave me such hope. Now I knew two people who had been healed through Pastor Wright's ministry. I spoke with Dana one day on the phone. She recommended that I read Corrie ten Boom's *The Hiding Place* and a biography of Smith-Wigglesworth. These books were a great inspiration.

I wanted to go to Pastor Wright's church immediately, but I had to wait. They could only accommodate one person at a time who needed major healing, and someone else was scheduled before me.[26]

---

[25] Pastor Henry Wright has taught "The 8 Rs to Freedom" which are: recognize, take responsibility, repent, renounce, remove, resist, rejoice, and restore.

[26] Since then the church has relocated to a larger facility in Thomaston, GA, and we accommodate large groups of people who come for the For My Life™ seminar.

Marcia bowling for the first time in 30 years - scored 91 points
8-21-92

Walk-out in St. Augustine, FL. Marcia wears a plastic raincoat and a
straw hat while on a diesel fueled trolley car. Anita in the background.
1992   Photo by Sharon Dawson

Anita Hill and Marcia, the healed of Lord, at Jacksonville
Beach, FL fulfilling Anita's vision. 1992

Parasailing in Hawaii 1993   Photo by Karen Stevens

Pastor Henry Wright baptizes Marcia. He was assisted by Cody Johnson.
Nellie Lower snaps the picture. 1995

Marcia, Bruce Gridley, and Anita Hill at Pleasant Valley Church
Thomaston, GA 1998

Marcia exhibiting her photograph at Slow Exposures
2006   Photo by Mary Cornelius

Marcia teaching at Be in Health™, a ministry of Pleasant Valley Church
2007   Photo by Linda Mcquiston

Chapter Thirteen

The Miracle Begins

Plans were finally made for me to fly to the East Coast on August 12, 1992. The airlines were having a price war so I got a really good deal. I made reservations on a midnight flight; as all people with E.I. know, there are less people wearing perfume and aftershave at night than in the morning. Because I had to change flights in St. Louis, I phoned ahead to the airport to inquire about their smoking policy. I was told that there was smoking only in designated areas. Everything was set. I had a prescription for oxygen from my doctor. I had ordered a wheelchair for the airport. I was ready to go!

My Christian friend drove me to the airport. Everything was an environmental challenge. I had no idea how I was to survive the trip, as I had not been away from my home except for a few hours at a time, with the exception of the meeting with the evangelist in San Francisco. I wasn't going to arrive at my destination until noon the next day. This was beyond my capabilities. I recall that when they closed the door of that airplane I was terrified. There was no way to get off!

The plane was almost sold out. We were sitting three across. The young man next to me took one look at me with all my gear and moved. Someone near me was wearing designer perfume, and I could smell it with my respirator on. I was trapped; there was no place to go. I was fervently praying, telling God that there was no way I could do this alone. Help! He had to help me; He had to do something. Please Father God!

The engines of the airplane were so loud. We hit some turbulence, and I took out my Sony Walkman and began listening to praise music. I had my respirator on, and I thought that no one could hear me with all the noise, so I started singing to myself. After about an hour I noticed that I could not smell the perfume anymore.

We landed in St. Louis and when they opened the door of the plane, there was a big rush of cigarette smoke. I didn't know what I was going to do. I had to get off to change planes. I discovered that smoking in designated areas meant that smoking was allowed on one side of the gate and not on the other side. Every gate had a smoking area. Smoke is particulate matter, and it goes right through a respirator. The miracle was that I did not react. I could smell the smoke but had no reaction *Nada, niente!* [27]

I was feeling pretty good by the time I got to my final destination. God had already met me, and for the first time I had been exposed to smoke without any reaction. No asthma, what a miracle! Although they had 4-5 bottles of oxygen for me per flight, I used less than one per flight.

Pastor Henry Wright, Anita, and two other ladies from the congregation met me at the airport, and we all piled into his vehicle. I was sitting in the front seat with Pastor and the others were in the back. The topic of conversation was Meshach, Shadrach, and Abednego in Daniel 3. I had never read Daniel, and I did not know what they were talking about. I thought they

---

[27] Spanish and Italian for nothing.

were being rude for ignoring me. As I looked back on this experience, I realized that they were holding me in the context of Scripture. I had just entered the fire, so to speak, and the LORD was there with me, just as He had been with them in the Bible.

Pastor, Anita, and the others decided that they wanted lunch; after all it was noon. Now, I had not been to a restaurant in six years. My diet was very restricted. I did not eat red meat, nor did I eat raw vegetables. I had not had any dairy, sugar or honey for about six years. I didn't eat fruit or wheat. I prepared my food in stainless steel cookware, and I used filtered water. What could I eat in a restaurant? Anita told me to go along with them, that they knew what they were doing. If it hadn't been for our friendship, I never would have trusted them. And she looked great. She was dressed up in a red top, a color that no E.I. person would ever wear. She was wearing cosmetics, a statement of health in itself.

The restaurant was smoky, and I had to take my respirator off in order to eat. I ordered a vegetarian pita melt from the menu; Pastor Henry ordered pizza, and it took them extra time to prepare it. I always remembered what Pastor had ordered, but I had to look at my journal of healing to see what I had ordered. While we were waiting for them to prepare the pizza, Pastor asked me if I wanted some prayer. I said, "Yes, please." He prayed a simple prayer coming against fear and stress, and I noticed that the cigarette smoke began to lift. The smell had been very oppressive. It was a brief period of time that it dissipated, a matter of a few minutes. I said, "Did they stop smoking in here?" He replied, "No, they are still smoking." When he said that, I could smell the smoke again.

You have to understand that my entire reality was one of smells. It is hard for a normal person to imagine what it is like when you are overwhelmed with a noxious smell, when your reality isn't anything but that smell. That is how it is with most people who have MCS/EI. They are hypersensitive in the area of smells, often in other areas too, such as noise or light. Bruce was different; he could not smell anything. He just reacted, not knowing what he was reacting to.

So the experience of the smell of the smoke fading into the background, even if only for a few minutes, was a miracle. And it gave me such hope that my illness could turn around quickly. It did not have to take a long time to be healed. God could do it instantly.

I had been awake now for over twenty-four hours, and we had church that night. I remember meeting the people in the congregation for the first time. This was the first group of Christians I had ever met. They seemed very different, not at all like my California friends. I enjoyed the praise and worship. One song made an impression on me. It was something about a horse and a rider being thrown into the sea. It did not make much sense, but I liked the song. Later I learned that this was the song of Moses praising God after having crossed the Red Sea.[28]

I met the woman who had come to the church before me for her healing. She was beautiful. Her hair was frosted; her makeup and clothes were impeccable. I knew that she had not looked that way when she first arrived. Look at me, wearing the one outfit I could tolerate with my industrial respirator on and my scarf babushka-style tied around my head. But I had hope that my appearance would change drastically as hers had.

---

[28] Exodus 15:1-2, 20-21

I was so tired, and Pastor Henry spoke for a very long time. It was torture for me to sit through the service. His topic was facts about the Bible, and I can even remember parts of the teaching. However, I thought he would never stop talking. Afterwards, we went to a small apartment that they named "The Samaritan." They had cleaned it the best they could to make it as allergen free as possible. On the dresser I put a large bag of homeopathic remedies and my new charcoal mask. Although I brought my remedies with me I did not use them. Praise the Lord!

Two ladies from the church were staying there with me. I did not know if I would be able to sleep because I had not slept on any bed other than my own for at least six years. I did strip the bedding and replace it with my own dirty sheets that I had not been able to wash. Often when I would lie down, my nervous system would vibrate, and I would feel like I was on a roller coaster; so I anticipated this being the case. Quite the opposite was true. I fell asleep with the two of them talking in the other room, and I slept like a baby all night.

The next morning I heard a noise in the bathroom, "pssssst." I immediately thought hair spray and I panicked. I could even smell hair spray through the closed door. I couldn't get away from it. My minister informed me that it was deodorant. Later they bought roll-on deodorant, but I was in and out of cerebral reactions all that day.

I was told to write down everything I took back and once having taken back my land, not to give it back to the Devil. (Refer to the Appendix C for the list of victories.)

That night someone from the congregation brought food for us. They served pork chops with black pepper. I had been a quasi-vegetarian for eighteen years, eating only occasional poultry or fish, because it was part of the lifestyle for those who followed the guru. I could not digest meat; I had tried.

My acupuncturist had told me that I was too yin, that E.I. was a yin disease, and that I needed to be more yang. Chinese medicine is based on balancing the yin and yang, which is a concept coming out of Taoism, an Eastern religion. So, in obedience to my practitioner, I tried red meat, but I could not digest it. I would be so tired afterward and in so much pain that I had to go to bed.

I told my ministers that, in no uncertain terms, could I eat pork chops. They said, "Yes you can. We'll pray for you." They prayed from 1 Timothy 4:1-4.

Now the Spirit speaketh expressly, that in the latter times some shall depart from the faith, giving heed to seducing spirits, and doctrines of devils; Speaking lies in hypocrisy; having their conscience seared with a hot iron; Forbidding to marry, and commanding to abstain from meats, which God hath created to be received with thanksgiving of them which believe and know the truth. For every creature of God is good, and nothing to be refused, if it be received with thanksgiving: For it is sanctified by the word of God and prayer.

The Holy Spirit gave me a revelation of this scripture, and I was blown away. It was amazing to me that God knew 2000 years ago that we would be vegetarian and that we would be celibate. Those who were serious about following the guru took vows of celibacy, poverty, and vegetarianism. But I saw from this scripture that God had created animals for us to eat. He did not like all the crazy, restrictive diets that I had been on: polarity diet, detoxification diets, macrobiotic diet, rotation diet, organic foods diet, etc. He wanted me to have my freedom. So, I took a few bites of the pork chop and I was okay. I did not have to go to bed. My stomach grumbled a little because it was not used to digesting pork, but I could live with that.

This was the beginning of my taking my foods back. I had not eaten dairy in six years; I had not eaten sugar or honey for just as long. I did not eat raw fruits or vegetables, because I had been following the macrobiotic diet. I was allergic to so many foods, but by the end of the week I was at a restaurant eating from the buffet: salads, raw vegetables, meat, dessert, dairy. I truly believe that normalizing my diet was foundational to my regaining my health. I had deprived myself of major food groups for many years, and it had taken a toll on my body.

The next day Pastor Henry came and began to teach me about the spirit, soul and body. His direction for me was that he wanted me to read the Bible every day. He told my ministry team not to pray deliverance for me. He discerned that I had so much of the occult in me that if they took it away, there would be nothing left. They could take authority over the spirits, mainly fear, and cancel its power over my life. Meanwhile I was to study Scripture.

On Sunday we had church; it lasted three hours. I reacted to the air conditioner and was miserable, sneezing and blowing my nose. We had church again in the evening with lots of praise music. I felt better when I was praising the Lord. I did not always understand the message, but I could relate to the music. And the Lord inhabits the praises of His people.[29] Music became an important part of my healing. I found that I always preferred the songs that directly quoted Scripture even when I had no idea the words were from the Bible.

---

[29] Psalm 22:3

The next day, I was driving with the ladies from my ministry team. They were talking in the front seat, and I felt left out. I thought they did not like me, and they did not want to be with me. They suggested that I try to take the respirator off, which I did. I was full of self-pity and rejection. When I verbalized that I did not fit in, the car was suddenly filled with car exhaust. The car had been O.K., and suddenly it was not O.K. They prayed for me and the symptoms left. This experience made a powerful impression on me; I saw how I had symptoms when I was feeling rejected. Now I could take my respirator off inside the car.

I began experimenting with different clothes. I was in the apartment with the window open for one hour. Over lunch we talked about the death of my father, and they ministered to me for the lack of forgiveness I had toward my mother for putting my father in the convalescent home. I continued to feel nauseous and dizzy. I thought I was reacting to the print in the Bible or to the clothes I was wearing. They said I had to take a stand against the Devil and not let him torment me. They told me that an evil spirit did not want me to read God's Word.

I realized that during certain topics of conversation I would have symptoms. I was uncomfortable talking about the antichrist, TV, movies, psychology, the guru, etc. I had a nightmare that night about Jim's abandonment of me. It was so real that I thought I was living it and woke up trembling. I cried a lot and received more prayer.

I had been there about a week when they had a going away party for the woman who had come to the ministry before me. The party was at a bowling alley, and it was filled with cigarette smoke. I had given up my mask, and no matter how uncomfortable I was, I did not put it back on. I bowled one game, long enough to have my picture taken with a bowling ball, and that was quite a victory. I spent the rest of the evening sitting outside in the car by myself while everyone else was bowling. I was into self-pity again thinking no one cared about me all alone in the car. Anita and I sent pictures of ourselves in the bowling alley to Bruce. This served as a wakeup call for him. He decided to contact the church himself and begin phone ministry.

I discovered that I did better when I was at church or a prayer meeting. I used these times to experiment with different clothes, makeup etc. I frequently sneezed in church. People told me that I was getting deliverance. I had no idea what was happening, but I was changing from day to day. I walked outside for several blocks without my respirator, quite a victory.

After being there two weeks they told me I was moving out of The Samaritan and over to Nellie's house. This was very threatening to me. I had just begun to feel secure where I was, and I was making progress. I did not want to move. Her house was large with several bedrooms. Anita was living there along with two young women. One of them smoked cigarettes, they both liked to wear perfume, and Nellie had dogs. I did not know how I would survive. I had reactions when I moved, but with prayer, I came out of them.

I finally had ministry time with Pastor Henry and his team. He told me that I did not fit the typical spiritual profile of someone with MCS/EI because I had not been abused as a child. He thought my broken heart had occurred later in life with all the disappointments, relationship failures, rejection and loss of love. He also said that I was the most analytical, critical, suspicious, mistrustful person he had ever met. He was obviously attacking my evil spirits. I had some rather ungodly thoughts about Pastor. I did not particularly like him; that is, my evil spirits did not like him, but I did not know the difference at that time.

I had a talk with Father God about Pastor Henry. I said, "I am here with this man to whom you have led me. He knows a lot about my illness and has helped others get their freedom. I don't like him. Please put a love in my heart for him. Give me love for Pastor Henry." And God answered that prayer and gave me a love and respect for him that has been consistent to this day.

Chapter Fourteen

Taking Back My Life

I went to a mall for the first time. Anita and two others were with me. The mall seemed like a very dark place with passageways going off in every direction. It reminded me of the souk in the Middle East. I was dizzy and nauseous, and my legs felt like lead. I felt as if I were being dragged from store to store. I thought I might die. Finally we were in a shop that sold hats. We were the only ones there, and we began to try on hats, the bigger, the more covered with net and bows, and brightly colored, the better. We laughed and laughed at ourselves. The clerk didn't quite know what to do with us. But after this my spirit rose up within me, and then we did some serious shopping. I bought some new clothes and a hat, and I wore the hat to church the next day. Great victory!

> **A merry heart doeth good like a medicine: but a broken spirit drieth the bones.**
> **Proverbs 17:22**

This was the scripture the Holy Spirit gave to Pastor Wright before he ministered to the first woman who was healed of Multiple Chemical Sensitivity, also known as Environmental Illness through his ministry.

Another thing I did to take back my life was to hang my clothes out to dry in the fresh air. Some days I would be O.K. with them, and other days I would react. Pastor Henry had told me that two steps forward and one step back, then three steps forward and two steps back were still forward progress. He said I should not give so much attention to reactions. They would pass if I didn't go into fear about them.

In mid September we went for an outing to St Augustine. We ate at a restaurant and looked into all the tourist shops. I was doing great; I felt normal. Then it started to rain so we took a city tour in an open-air electric cable car, and we were subjected to the elements including car exhaust from other vehicles. I was wearing a plastic poncho and a straw hat, two things that I could never have tolerated before. It was a challenge but I hung in. On the way home I started wheezing. They prayed for me, and the shortness of breath went away. It never ceased to amaze me how symptoms could be turned around so quickly with prayer.

One day Nellie took me with her to an opening of a large discount store that was housed in a warehouse. I had cerebral reactions. Now, I never went anywhere without my Bible with me so while she was off shopping, I took my Bible out right there in the middle of the store and started reading until I could get the reaction to subside. Another time we were out shopping with friends hitting all the stores: Kmart, Wal-Mart, Target etc. I became very fatigued, and I did not think I could take another step. I decided to sit in an outdoor café while they went into another store. I was so tired I laid my head down on the table and I told myself:

I can do all things through Christ which strengtheneth me. Philippians 4:13

My energy returned. I felt renewed in the Lord, and I went in yet another store and shopped for another hour.

This was the bottom line truth for me. The whole time I had followed the guru I became more sensitive, more isolated, and more miserable. Since I had given my life to Jesus my world had been expanding, and I had life more abundantly. I had no desire to go back to my old lifestyle.

> **The thief cometh not but to steal, and to kill, and to destroy: I am come that they might have life, and that they might have it more abundantly. John 10:10**

I had originally thought I would be perfectly content if I could wear clothes, go outside without a mask, and eat whatever food I wanted. I had achieved all this in a relatively short amount of time, and yet I was depressed. When I told Pastor Henry that I was depressed, he prayed against depression, death, divination, pharmakeia, and an antichrist spirit. I felt at peace after that.

I have often said that getting well was one of the most difficult things I have ever had to do. Many don't understand why and don't want to hear that it takes work to walk out of spiritual bondage. I had given up the guru, and I had reached out to Jesus Christ, but I was still in a transitional stage. All the antichrist spirits were fighting to keep me on their side. There was a war in the heavens on my behalf. But fortunately it is God's battle, and we do not have to do it by ourselves. In fact, it is impossible to win this battle in our own power.

Pastor Henry gave a teaching that he called "The Seven Steps to Sin." Sin begins in the mind with thought. Evil thoughts are not necessarily sin; they represent temptation. You do not have to repent for temptation if you do not follow it. I realized that I had been tortured by my thoughts, and they were not my thoughts to begin with. The enemy gave them to me trying to tempt me. I could now separate myself from these thoughts; they were not mine.[30] I felt liberated, and my headache miraculously left. The truth can make you free.

Pastor had told me that we do not always need deliverance. We can turn our back and walk away from our sins. He said that I would be so filled up with the Word of God that there would no more room for the evil spirits, and they would have to leave. I have witnessed in other people's lives when they turned away from false religions, occult practices, etc., that the Lord reversed their environmental illness also. What He has done for me, He will do for you because He does not play favorites.

. . . Of a truth I perceive that God is no respecter of persons: Acts 10:34

There was no TV or newspapers in Nellie's house where I was living. So I would go to the library to read the newspaper. I checked out a library book that I was secretly enjoying, but felt guilty about reading. Then one day I discovered a small TV hidden in her bedroom, and I would sneak in there when she was at work and watch my favorite soap opera. However, in spite of my rebellion, God was delivering me and healing me.

I was falling out of agreement with the guru's meditation. I had practiced these techniques for so many years that I would automatically go into silent meditation when presented with certain triggers. I had to consciously stop myself. The same happened with birthdates. I automatically would think of the astrological meaning of dates. That was another habit that required some work and a measure of time to

---

[30] Pastor Henry W. Wright has a teaching entitled "Separation" in which he teaches these important principles.

break the habit. I had to catch the thought every time and cast it down according to 2 Corinthians 10:5.

> **Casting down imaginations, and every high thing that exalteth itself against the knowledge of God, and bringing into captivity every thought to the obedience of Christ.**

I had to be careful that while I was stretching not to do any yoga exercises. Many Christians do not understand that yoga comes out of Hinduism, and the exercises are designed to awaken Kundalini. Kundalini literally means serpent power. This power resides at the base of the spine, and it rises through the various chakras (energy centers) along the spine, bringing demonic psychic power and "union with god" with it. Kundalini is really just another word for divination. I was taught that we could not separate the spirituality from the practice, and that the practice is an expression of the spirituality. This is true for yoga, martial arts, Chinese medicine, etc., which all come out of eastern religions.

Reading through the New Testament was a challenge for me. I often did not understand what I was reading. When one has been into the occult there are antichrist spirits that come along to make reading the Bible difficult. I would become sleepy, had trouble concentrating, and it would not make sense to me. I was a person with a master's degree, yet the teenage high school dropout who lived with us would have to explain Scripture to me. She understood it and I did not.

One day I asked Pastor Henry if it were possible to be a Christian and also be a Democrat. He said yes, but I should realize that the Democrats aligned themselves with sin, namely, abortion and homosexuality. When we have unrepentant sin, whether personally or as a nation, it opens the door to the enemy who now has a legal right to persecute us. I asked him to teach me about abortion. He said that conception begins in the heart of God first and that we should not tamper with God's creation. He referred me to Psalm 139 and Jeremiah 1.

> **For thou hast possessed my reins: thou hast covered me in my mother's womb. I will praise thee: for I am fearfully and wonderfully made: marvelous are thy works; and that my soul knoweth right well. My substance was not hid from thee, when I was made in secret, and curiously wrought in the lowest parts of the earth. Thine eyes did see my substance, yet being unperfect; and in thy book all my members were written, which in continuance were fashioned, when as yet there was none of them. Psalms 139: 13-16**

> **Before I formed thee in the belly I knew thee; and before thou camest forth out of the womb I sanctified thee, and I ordained thee a prophet unto the nations. Jeremiah 1:5**

After reading Psalm 139 I repented to God for my abortion. Afterward I felt very ill: dizzy, nauseated and burping. I also felt tremendous grief and sadness. God was delivering me of my sin.

Living and working in the San Francisco bay area had put me into contact with many gay and lesbian people. Many of them became friends; some were my supervisors. The commonality in many of the women's lives was that they had been terribly abused by men: fathers, brothers and/or husbands. This caused them to choose an alternative lifestyle that is contrary to God's Word. They need the Lord just as the rest of us do. I learned that there is no hierarchy in sin. Whether it is abortion, gossip, anger, murder, unforgiveness, fear, or homosexuality, it is all sin.

Pastor Henry also told me that I should not turn my back on the enemy, ignore him or turn away. I must do battle; that is spiritual warfare. I must take a stand. We should also speak aloud to the enemy. He does not read our thoughts. Declaring silently to God is not nearly as effective as declaring out loud our intention so that the enemy can hear it also.

One day Anita had a word for me. She said that she thought the medic alert bracelet I wore chained me to my illness. It was a label or a curse that I was wearing. I felt convicted, so after a little prayer I took the bracelet off and threw it into the garbage.[31] We then set out for the Dollar Store. We had to walk down a very busy street with lots of traffic, including large trucks. We hung out at the Dollar Store a long time trying on clothes, etc. I felt entirely normal; it was wonderful!

The very next day Anita and another friend went out for lunch. I was not included, and I felt very rejected. That afternoon I went to the new laundromat in town. The previous week I had gone to an older one and had used the machines, including the gas dryer and had been O.K., but that day I had one of the worst cerebral reactions that I had experienced since arriving at the church. The reaction lasted for a long time, and I had to lie down. I prayed for myself, and Nellie prayed for me. After awhile the cerebral reactions lifted, but I felt very depressed. They had returned from lunch by then. When I told them about the depression they did some very strong praying and it left. How could something be so profound in one minute and gone the next? Only God could make that happen.

In retrospect, I thought of this reaction as retaliation by the devil[32] for the absolutely normal day

---

[31] This is not to be construed as advice but merely my testimony. I am not recommending that anyone else throw their medic alert bracelet away.

[32] I say devil, but I mean an evil spirit. There is only one Devil, and he is not omnipresent.

I had the day before, so I have realized that when I have had a great victory with the Lord, the attack soon follows. But when I read my diary, I realized that I had fallen into agreement with a spirit of rejection, and that started the chain reaction of cerebral symptoms followed by fatigue and then profound depression. It had been rejection, instead of retaliation, that had given me the reactions.

Anita and I planned to go to Jacksonville Beach. We wanted to walk on the beach to fulfill the vision Anita had had in California. The day we set aside to go, I woke up sneezing and blowing my nose with terrible allergic-type reactions. I was so sick that I did not want to go anywhere, but they insisted I go and told me that the devil did not want me to fulfill the vision. As soon as I got in the car the reactions lifted, and I had no more problems the rest of the day. We spent an hour walking on the beach while our driver had a dentist appointment. We took photographs to commemorate that day. One of them is on the cover of this book.

When Anita and I were talking about this in California, we had no idea that God would make this come true at a beach on the Atlantic coast instead of the Pacific. I also learned that the enemy would try to prevent me from doing something that God wanted me to do, but once I took the step in faith, then the enemy would give up.

We can passively wait for God to heal us, and nothing will happen. It is only when we step out in faith that God meets us. I had also experienced that on the airplane coming to the ministry.

One morning I woke up to the smell of Clorox and Pine-Sol. When I went downstairs, Nellie was on her hands and knees scrubbing the kitchen floor. This was after I had made a comment about the floor being

140

dirty the day before. I freaked out, ran up the stairs, and slammed the bedroom door after me. She and Anita were right behind me. I shouted at them to close the door, but they would not. They commanded spirits of fear and control to come out of me.

I was asked when the fear of suffocation first came in. I remembered a mask of ether being put over my face before having my tonsils removed. I was four years old when that occurred. That was the open door, or one of them, when the spirit of fear came into me. There was also the time my mother hit me across the back and knocked the wind out of me when I was screaming my head off. That was during WWII when we were alone. They cast that fear out, and afterwards, the reaction went down and I was okay with the smell.

Chapter Fifteen

Healing through Ministry

My first official ministry session with Pastor Henry occurred in November. On the actual day of the appointment I felt great, no problems in the world. No evil spirits were tormenting me. I think they were hiding from Pastor Henry.

I knew that fear and occultism were the two spiritual legs that MCS/EI stood on. At a later time Pastor Henry also said it was all held in place by self-pity.

I made a long list of all the spirits I thought I had allowed into my being. I told Pastor that I wanted to get rid of all of them except one, and that was an intellectual spirit. I was afraid that when it went, I would lose my intelligence. He said that would not be the case, but we could wait on that one. I had given it much thought, and I felt that the occultism was the big one needing to be addressed. Pastor made the same decision, and we were in agreement. After all, I had been walking out my fears for some time.

We first talked about doubt and unbelief as Pastor Henry had been teaching a series on faith Wednesday nights. <u>I had to get doubt out of my mind before I could receive from God.</u> Doubt and unbelief are related to fear, and doubt and unbelief had kept the Hebrews from entering the Promise Land.

> **And to whom sware he that they should not enter into his rest, but to them that believed not? So we see that they could not enter in because of unbelief. Hebrews 4:18-19**

Pastor Henry exhorted me not to be intimidated by the mountain of my problems and the smallness of my faith. He said the following:

Whether you have fear or faith, it is your decision. Which one will you believe? In MCS/EI you are not sensitive to chemicals, but you are sensitive to fear. Fear says you will react, and faith says you will not react.

Now faith is the substance of things hoped for, the evidence of things not yet seen.
Hebrews 11:1

Fear is the opposite of that; it is the substance of things not hoped for. Fear destroys all the good. Fear says it will never happen, but faith always defeats fear. You find your place in it by decision. <u>Faith is an act of your will</u>. You must make a decision not to be afraid. Choose to believe in God and have faith.

The exhortation went on:

You can defeat fear without having to cast it out. We must be careful that in our fear we think we must always do deliverance. There is something that God wants to do in our hearts as an act of our will because of our faith. In the days to come, you will tell me all the reasons why it is not happening. It will be because it has not happened yet, or because of all the symptoms, or thoughts that say it is not going to happen. Faith has got to come forth, not mind over matter or positive thinking, but because you believe in spite of the circumstances.

If you have pain, do not deny it, but do not take finality in what is, because then you eliminate what can be. Pain is a statement of what is, not a statement of what can be. Do not lose hope. People who give up the will to

144

live, they die, not because anything killed them, but because they gave up. They lost hope.

You do not deny your reality; you just do not accept it. Do you accept the finality of death and disease? If we do, then there is no place for ministry. God transcends death and disease. God transcends failure. God transcends fear and torment.

We all have a measure of faith. Faith is a growing thing. Faith is as the mustard seed. Faith produces change for the better. Faith always produces solutions. Now the mountain of your illness over-shadows the seed of your faith. Satan reminds you of how big he is through your symptoms, but God can move a mountain into the sea. How do you get more faith? By reading the Word.

So then faith comes by hearing and hearing by the word of god. Romans 10:17

I know the mountain in your life is greater than your mustard seed of faith. But a mustard seed is like nuclear energy. It is very strong.

In your heart you know how you would like to be. You have just engaged the greatest architect. He designed you. His name is God. He designed you before you were ever born. Satan has come and said, "No, you can't be what he created you to be." Allow God to remove certain things and to restore you.

Occult spirits will always interfere. They don't agree and they are negative. You are going to have to believe God, His Word, and believe me and not listen to the voices in your mind. God would say, "According to your faith, so be it unto you."

Pastor Henry has talked about this ministry session. He said he was ministering to an astrologer who wanted to convert him to astrology. After this exhortation on faith, we had a discussion about astrology, and I wanted to understand why God did not want me to have this information. <u>Pastor told me that the degree to which I hold on to ungodly things, that is the degree to which Satan has power over my life</u>. I knew from His Word that people who practice astrology are an abomination to God.[33] That was enough for me to stop the practice, but I had to understand why.

Pastor Henry was very patient and listened to my arguments. He was silently speaking to God asking what to say, and asking how he could get through to me. Finally, he told me not to be bound to the physical world of creation. I should not limit myself by reality, even if it were true; I should be able to go beyond reality. The LORD created the heavens and earth. He called things into being that were not. Why would I limit myself to the negative prognostications of astrology? I began to get some understanding.

He told me that the Devil had a plan for my life, and so did God. Astrology and other means of divination map out the Devil's plan. <u>Why would I settle on the creation when I could have the Creator? When I accepted the finality of what is, I eliminated what could be.</u> Why would I accept the finality of disease? I had a revelation of this. I wanted the Creator who could change things instantly. Was this not a more excellent way?[34]

---

[33] Deuteronomy 18:10-12.

[34] I have an audiotape of this session and Pastor Wright did say this. He has since written a book entitled *A More Excellent Way*™. We no longer tape any ministry session at Pleasant Valley Church.

Pastor taught me that the occult is the counterfeit of God. It represented the antichrist in my life. Divination, which is a religious spirit, had come and been as real as the Holy Spirit. It was the counterfeit and hid the one true and living God. The only way anyone can tell the difference between divination and the Holy Spirit is by comparing it to Scripture or through a word from God.

Pastor prayed a simple prayer; he declared that the power of the occult be diminished in my life. He also prayed that God would shed His light into my darkness. He released the Spirit of God into my life. I did not have any physical manifestation, nor did he experience anything in the physical. It was several years later when Pastor Donna Wright delivered me from spirits of divination and chiropractic that I had a physical manifestation following the deliverance, and I was convinced that both were evil.

After this first session with Pastor Henry, I had a time of repentance; I repented for just about every sin I could remember, including the drugs and the sex. I continued to have reactions, but I also had victory.

I noticed that the cerebral symptoms that had plagued me for so long were starting to disappear. I made a connection between the symptoms and the prayer taking authority over occultism in my life that Pastor had prayed. Soon after, I ventured out to go to the mall by myself. I drove down the street to the intersection. If I turned right, I would be headed toward the grocery store. If I turned left, I would be headed out of town. I made the left turn and immediately I began to feel dizzy and nauseous. I said out loud, "Evil spirit, I see what you are trying to do. I am going to the mall and you will not stop me." I continued on my way in a battle with the enemy, but he did not deter me. I went to the mall, did my shopping, and returned home.

I had another session with Pastor about a week later. I had discovered the proverb that said:

He that hath no rule over his own spirit is like a city that is broken down and without walls.
Proverbs 25:28

I told Pastor Henry that this was what was wrong with me. I was like a broken down city that didn't have walls. I took in whatever was around me. I had no boundaries. He pointed out that that was because I did not rule my own spirit. When one has a broken heart, it is fragmented, and evil spirits of bitterness, rejection and self-rejection, self-hatred, fear and occultism come in. Ministry was about getting my heart healed. Jesus came to heal the broken-hearted.

In this ministry session we dealt with family issues and sexual sin. We had been looking for the open door, how a spirit of promiscuity got entrance into my life in the first place. Most sins come down through the generations as inherited iniquities. I knew that my father had been promiscuous. I had telephoned my mother to see if there was anything in family history that I did not know about. She told me about her molestation; she was about four years old at the time. She said the man did not hurt her, but because he was a friend of her father it happened more than once. She never told her parents. This could be the inherited spirit of sexual victimization.

I confessed my personal sin before Pastor and his ministry partner, and I was filled with so much shame. Pastor Henry talked to God on my behalf. Because I have a recording of this conversation I have reproduced it, and I believe you may get your freedom from this teaching and prayer. But repent for your sins first. Forgive anyone you are holding unforgiveness toward. You can put your name in this prayer where my name is.

Pastor Henry spoke:

> Marcia, the spiritual dynamics of your life are starting to be recognized. The things you have done and where you have been are the product of a satanic plan to destroy you through people who also have a demonic lifestyle.
>
> Everything you have ever done, that you feel shame for, you have to lay it down at the feet of the Lord and walk away from it without your shame. You cannot relive it. Satan will try to bring you back into it. Take your freedom from shame. I don't condemn you. The Lord does not condemn someone in sin. He simply asks them to deal with it. Recognize the reality and source of it. Go into a place of freedom with Him that you never had before.
>
> I don't judge you after evil spirits or after your failures. I am judging you after where God wants to take you. He wants to take you out of that quagmire of hell where you finally lay it down: the people, the hurts, the men, the women, the hell and understand why they were the way they were. Why you are the way you are as a person has nothing to do with the way God created you. I must bring you to a place somehow, past all the demonics, past all the familiars, past all the inheritance and bring you before the Lord. And God would say I have been waiting for you. Now pick up and go on. Somehow, we have to come to that to get your heart healed.
>
> God does not condone sin, but he is in the middle of it to heal and deliver and direct. I must bring you to that place of mercy and grace. Yes, you won't forget, but you will know

149

why you got there, and you will know that you were a victim. I know that there were things beyond you. Even if you sin tomorrow, you bring yourself back before His feet and you lay it out before him and take your forgiveness and forgive the others.

Any demon in Hell that is interfering, I break their power because they are lying, accusing spirits that are in place to reinforce their reality in your life. I must break that. I speak to the evil spirits and say ENOUGH. Her problems are none of your business. I want this woman free. Their days are numbered. I have got to get you separated somehow so that you as a spirit can go on.

Your broken heart is a work of Satan. I am trying to get your spirit free where you can take your peace between you and God. I ask the Lord to do that for you now. God can instantly come and make the lame man walk. It doesn't have to be drawn out. If I could speak that into you right now and mend your heart, and set you free from all the condemnation and guilt, and give you the heart of a butterfly that would rise again out of your hell and take your freedom, I would do it. I do do it in the name of Jesus.

All the familiar spirits, all the inherited spirits, all the curses, all the unclean, unloving spirits, rejected spirits, fear spirits, all the rest of them that came in, all the soul ties. I would put them under the blood by my spoken word because that is what Christ is capable of doing. Just like that. Their power is broken. If I could speak that into you, Marcia, in the name of Jesus and create that reality and break their power once and for all, I would do it. I would set you free from your torment. I would give you your life back in the name of Jesus. I would set you free. If God would honor my words, I would do it just for you. Lord, would you do it for her? Would you cause the flood to roll out of her? God's sheep has been a victim of the Devil long enough. I don't condemn her. You did not come to condemn us. You came that we might have freedom through your life.

I am not her judge. Lord, you are not her judge. You are her deliverer. Without you, Lord, there is no hope for any of us. We are all evil. Every single one of us is evil apart from you. Would you free us? Give us our life back. Would you deliver my sister from her devils? Would you do that, Lord? Would you do that for Marcia? Would you allow the floodgates to bust open and all this hell be dispersed with light, all the shame and guilt and condemnation? Please, Sir, would you do that for my sister?

Father, I ask you in the name of Jesus, just as the compassion of the Spirit is so strong here; LORD, I ask you to be a Lord to her. Father, I ask you to be a father to her. Jesus, I ask you to be a spiritual husband to her. God, I ask that you heal her. You can take the pain away. You can take fear away. You can take all of this away. Would you touch her, God? Would you do that for my sister? I want it for her. Reach down from heaven, touch her spirit and touch her soul. Set things in order in her heart. Give her peace. The compassion of the Lord is so strong here.

God knows your heart, Marcia. He knows the highways you have traveled. Your life is not finished. Your book is not finished. I refuse to release you to Satan. I want you to have peace. It's not that you won't have a few emotions, a few little fears. I want the torment gone. I want you to have a sense of direction and a sense of purpose that has nothing to do with anyone else. Another man's presence is not your source of love. There is a love that transcends, that comes to your bosom that comes from God where you can accept yourself and have peace with yourself, whether your mama likes you, or your daddy likes you, or whether your best friend betrays you, whatever.

We don't judge people after devils. We judge them after the order of creation as God sees it. I judge you that way. I know God created you; you are not an accident. I think you might make a statement that can change the direction of a person's life.

Your thinking is being reordered. It is painful but it is okay. I want God to heal your broken heart. Where you are going is what excites me, not where you have come from. The woman caught in adultery, the religious leaders said, "Stone her." The Word says to stone her. Jesus said, "He who is without sin, cast the first stone." When everyone had left, he said, "Sister, neither do I condemn you. Go your way and sin no more."[35] It was a need to be loved and accepted that caused the woman to sin. A need to be loved and accepted is a basic root of all mankind.

---

[35] John 8:11

My job is to represent the Lord to you, His will and His love. It is not that you are free of sin that is the issue; that is not the critical issue at the moment. What you are doing with your sins is the critical issue. It is an attitude of the heart that the Lord is concerned about. It isn't your righteousness or the absence of sin he is concerned about. It is His righteousness and where you are finding yourself in it. He knows the ways of men. The Lord's provision is to take things one at a time. Satan will come along and show you all of your sins at one time.

For if our heart condemn us, God is greater than our heart, and knoweth all things. 1 John 3:20

The immediate need is for God to heal your heart. I want God to do something so sovereignly that you can't give me credit for it.

The intensity of the Spirit was so powerful at that moment. I knew Pastor did not set me free, because it was when I called out to God in my heart to forgive me and free me from the torment of guilt and shame that He answered me. It just all disappeared. He heard me crying out to Him. I knew it was the Lord who set me free. I could lay my burden down and walk away.

But God, who is rich in mercy, for his great love wherewith he loved us, Even when we were dead in sins, hath quickened us together with Christ, (by grace ye are saved;) And hath raised us up together, and made us sit together in heavenly places with Christ Jesus: That in the ages to come he might shew the exceeding riches of his grace in his kindness toward us through Christ Jesus. Ephesians 2:4-7

Chapter Sixteen

Returning Home

During the week following this powerful ministry session I was scheduled to fly to Indiana to meet my mother and visit her family whom I had not seen in fifteen years. I was calm that morning until my friend picked me up to take me to the airport. We had to wait in the airport for one and one half hours because the plane was late. I was very nervous about leaving. I was having reactions to the airport because of my fear. When I finally was allowed to board, she walked me to the airplane door praying deliverance from fear the whole way until she gave me a little push, and I was on my own.

The plane was very crowded, and it seemed like many people were wearing perfume. I wanted my mask! My instruction had been not to give ground to the enemy. Since I had given up my mask, I should not pick it up again. We made a stop in the Carolinas, and I did not get off. I stood by the open door that was letting in fresh air with one of the stewardesses. I mentioned that there had been a lot of perfume in the plane. She agreed wholeheartedly, and as we talked I realized that she had chemical sensitivities also. I shared my testimony how only three and a half months ago I had flown from California with oxygen and a mask. I told her how I had been healed through Jesus Christ.

And they overcame him by the blood of the Lamb and the word of their testimony; and they loved not their lives unto the death. Revelation 12:11

My mother and my aunt met me at the airport. On the way in the car I was eager to talk about my experience of healing, but my mother kept interrupting me. She definitely wanted to change the subject.

When we arrived at the house I was taken to the room I was to use. It had been my cousin's, and she recently married and moved out. She had smoked cigarettes, and the residue was throughout the house. I panicked. I telephoned the church and they prayed for me. I came into peace, and the smell in the house dissipated and did not bother me the rest of the visit.

I had many environmental challenges on this trip: my uncle's brand new van, linens washed in regular detergent and fabric softener, restaurants, gymnasiums, and temperatures close to zero. We even attended a concert of Christmas music in a large auditorium filled with people. One evening we went to a Chinese restaurant, and when we walked in I was hit with a strong chemical smell due to their remodeling. The E.I. spirit took over. I was very angry with the proprietors, and I had lots of fear. I was in a major battle, but I hung in until the meal was over.

Walking out of an illness is not about it being easy! It has more to do with drawing a line against the enemy and saying, "No more are you going to rob me of my life. I am taking back my land." When you make a decision that you are going to do something in spite of symptoms and follow through with it, the enemy discovers that he can't use you as a means of expression anymore, and he will take his leave.

It was a revelation to me that my family was not interested in how I had been healed by God. There was one exception, and that was my Uncle Don. He wanted to hear all about it. He had been raised in the church, and he had been a soloist in church all of his adult life. He found my testimony to be a wonderful example of

God's healing power. My mother was very quiet, and she listened to every word while I told him about it.

The return trip on the airplane was very smooth. I continued to witness to my old friends through notes on Christmas cards. I sent cards to my New Age practitioners, my Buddhist friends, my Unity minister, my therapist and my friend who followed the guru and told them of the wonderful healing I had experienced through the ministry of Jesus Christ. I wrote in my card to Bruce, "After my trip to Indiana, I can truly say I am healed. The trip back was so much easier than going out, and I called back here frequently for prayer. And every time God answered our prayer, and I broke through to a new level. I rode in my uncle's brand new van, and stayed in a smoke-filled house, and used towels dried in scented Bounce, went to a concert, three restaurants, a basketball game and am here to tell the tale."

In a subsequent ministry session with Pastor Henry, he taught me about the kingdom of Satan and how it is organized. He had toy soldiers spread over his desk. He pointed to one and said, "This is the general. He is the principality. Here are the officers under him, the corporals, the sergeants, the majors, etc. And over here are the privates. They are the little guys. You never hear of the general getting killed; it happens to the little guys under him. They are in place to protect the general. In order to get to the general you have to defeat the privates and the officers first, and then the general is exposed. In spiritual warfare we go after the underlings first before casting out the principality."

He said that my symptoms came out of fear. Under the principality of fear there are some major fears that most people have to address: fear of dying, fear of failure, fear of man, and fear of rejection.

Under these we have individual fears; for example: fear of being in crowds, fear of snakes, fear of mothers-in-law, fear of lightning, and in my case, fear of wind, etc. We defeat the little guys one by one, then we go after the bigger ones, and finally the principality of fear is exposed without any defenses, and now we can defeat him.

Pastor Henry has a favorite expression about spiritual warfare. He says that most people shadow box with the enemy, and that does no good. We need to be specific about our enemy. If it is a fear of abandonment, then let's focus on that issue. Let's recognize it in our life and let us take personal responsibility for it. Then we can repent for it, renounce it and remove it from our life.[36] But to say that we are defeating Satan in our lives means very little. Get rid of those privates, those underlings first.

On New Year's Day January 1, 1993, I fasted. I had not been able to fast when I was ill because I had problems with hypoglycemia. This time I dedicated the time to the Lord because I wanted a closer relationship with Him. As a result of this fast I received some insight regarding my healing. As long as I was focused on the healing rather than the Healer, the healing remained out of my grasp. But when I gave up the healing and focused on the Healer, God the Father, making Him the more important one in my life, the healing came forth. Also, it was after I had stopped the striving and driveness to find the natural remedy that worked, when I laid it all down, all the herbs, diets, homeopathic remedies, weekly chiropractic appointments, etc., that the healing began.

I was scheduled to return to California in early February. On the morning of my departure I had a

---

[36] Pastor Wright has a teaching on the 8 R's to freedom.

session with Pastor Henry. He delivered me of every spirit that had been on my list. I got on an airplane in Florida, and flew to St. Louis. This time I did not smell the cigarette smoke in the airport. Yes, they still smoked at each gate on one side, but it did not bother me.

Without a wheelchair as before, I walked to the gate where I was to board the plane for San Francisco. What I noticed were the passengers. In Florida everyone was conservatively and neatly dressed. Here, there was such a conglomeration of people, different ethnic groups and races, people of different sexual persuasions, casual and often weird dress, tattoos, men wearing earrings, pastel colored hair, etc. These people represented San Francisco, California. I thought to myself, "Is this where I belong? Does this represent me?" This contrast from where I had come to where I was going was clear.

The plane taxied out to the end of the runway and there we sat. They were revving up the engines, and I could smell the diesel fuel in the air conditioning. Time passed ever so slowly. My chest started to tighten, and I feared that the asthma was returning. I looked across the aisle, and there sat a man reading his Bible, the book of Revelation to be exact. How often on an airplane to San Francisco do you find a man reading his Bible? I don't recall such a happening either before or after this flight. I didn't care who he was or what denomination he was. My only thought was I have to ask this guy for prayer. I introduced myself and gave him a brief testimony and told him I was having problems with shortness of breath. I asked him to pray for me. He did and I felt better. My fear level had decreased. For most of the flight I visited with this gentleman, telling him where I had come from and all that God had done for me. The only thing I remember about him was that he went to the Church of the Nazarene.

Would God meet me in California away from the church? I was unsure if my healing would hold fast in California. It worked on the East Coast, but was it portable? I would soon find out.

The spring had been the most difficult season for me. I had many allergies, first to the trees, then the flowers, and finally, the grasses. Besides respiratory flu symptoms I would be very fatigued, spending much time in bed. This year was different; I could hold my own. I continued to walk out from my issues and my illness.

I made an appointment with my psychotherapist to witness to him. Anyone who had known me when I was ill would be able to see such a change in my countenance. I did not have to tell them I was healed; they could see it. In any case, I witnessed to him that I was not allergic to the pollens this spring, and that my healing was real in California also.

An hour or so later I was taking a walk at Lake Merritt just in time for the feeding of the birds, the pigeons and the pelicans. The pigeons that had been on the ground took flight *en masse*, and they hovered about ten feet in the air, hundreds of them. Their little wings were fluttering, and I could see dust and pollen raining down from overhead. Oh no, I was being dusted with pollen. Was this retaliation because I had shared testimony that I was healed of pollen allergies? I did not know, but it seemed very coincidental. I prayed a fervent prayer against fear of reacting and fear of pollen and was fine.

I went through my apartment getting rid of all objects that were even remotely related to the occult.

Neither shall thou bring an abomination into thine house, lest thou be a cursed thing like it: but thou shalt utterly detest it, and thou shalt utterly abhor it; for it is a cursed thing. Deuteronomy 7:26

I threw away one hundred fifty astrology books, my file of astrological charts, pictures of the guru, and books on psychic and naturopathic healing. I sold my radionics machine to a friend who already had one and wanted another; later I regretted that decision and realized that I should have busted it up and thrown it away.

I had a collection of jewelry from the Middle East: Egypt, Turkey, India, and Iran. I got rid of the pieces that were obviously from another religion, the hands of Fatima, the inverted moons, scarabs, etc. I kept a pendant that I had purchased in Nepal. It was a beautiful silver piece with gold filigree and big hunks of turquoise and coral. One day, I put it on and I got so dizzy and nauseous; something came over my mind. This was a total shock to me because I used to wear this jewelry when I was sick and had no problem with it whatsoever.

On Telegraph Avenue in Berkeley near the university, there was a little shop called Katmandu. I took the pendant there to show it to the proprietor. I told her that I had purchased it in Katmandu, Nepal. What could she tell me about it? She looked at it, turned it over, and said, "This is the sign of the ohm. This is a Buddhist piece." She took it apart and continued, "They put the written prayers in here." I felt like such a fool. I knew what the sign of the ohm looked like; in fact I had embroidered it on a shirt for a friend of mine. How could I have looked at that engraving and not recognized it?

161

My 1930's Webster's Dictionary says that the occult means concealed, to cover over, hidden from the eye or understanding, mysterious, invisible, secret. In other words, something can be right before your face, and yet you don't see it. That was my experience with the pendant. Also, I had done a very thorough cleaning of my apartment, ridding my space of any occult object. Yet months later, I found a picture of the guru at the bottom of a drawer. It had escaped my attention the first time around. I believe this is very typical of the occult because the occult is deceptive.

After I had been home for several months, I awoke one morning and had severe dizziness on one side of my head. I could not stand up. I felt as if I had a giant magnet on the left side of my head that was drawing my head down to the ground. I held on to the walls as I staggered to the bathroom. I barely made it back to bed, and I telephoned my friend in Florida. She began doing warfare against occult spirits. After a time of fierce deliverance prayer the dizziness started to lift, never to return. I danced around my apartment singing the third Psalm.

But thou, O LORD, art a shield for me; my glory and the lifter of mine head. Psalms 3:3

162

Chapter Seventeen

More Walk-out

I had not been home for very long when my Christian friend took me to a conference with a well-known Bible teacher. While I was sitting in the audience, I kept thinking that the church seemed familiar to me. Then I remembered that this was the church where I had the confrontation with David's ex-wife. My friend and I attended this church on Sunday, and they had a healing service. The founder of the church, Pastor Violet Kiteley, laid hands on me and prayed for me at this service. I took this to be a sign that this was the church for me. David's ex-wife was surprised to see me, but she believed it to be an answer to prayer as she had prayed for my salvation.

My entire experience with the guru had been one of turning inward, silently meditating. Even in large crowds of devotees it would be quiet because we would be meditating. Shiloh Christian Fellowship was at the opposite end of the spectrum. They were a large Pentecostal-style church where everything was loud. I liked that because it was not like anything I had experienced before.

I began attending Shiloh regularly, but a short time later they did some refurbishing, laying down new carpets. I was very disappointed, as I believed that I had to stay away because of the fumes emitted from the new rugs. I did not go to church for several weeks where in the past it would have been for many months or maybe even a year, but I know better now how to face my fears and not let them rule my life.

I was so in love with the Lord and His church that I wanted to experience every aspect of Christianity. I visited many churches throughout the Bay Area, and whenever I heard that they had a nationally known guest speaker I would be there. I consider myself very blessed that I was able to hear many people speak: Marilyn Hickey, Oral Roberts, Benny Hinn, George Otis Jr., Dick Eastman, Phil Driscoll, John Wimber, John Bevere, Ed Silvoso, Joyce Meyer, Mario Murillo, Ken Clement, Bret Kjos. The list goes on. Some Sundays I would attend services in three different churches. The Holy Spirit was teaching me and giving me discernment through all these experiences.

A visiting evangelist, Mahesh Chavda, who was an Indian man from Africa, was speaking at several Chinese churches in San Francisco, and I attended one of the meetings. What made this service so unique was that the evangelist spoke English with an Indian accent, and the interpreter translated him into Chinese. The praise songs were sung in both English and Chinese. I thought it might be a good idea if Bruce came to one of the healing services. I contacted his phone minister to ask if this was wise, and she agreed, so I invited Bruce to come to a meeting. He drove in his car separate from me, because he wanted to be able to escape if need be.

Bruce was dressed in a white, sweat outfit. He wore an industrial respirator as I used to do. He had on white cotton gloves because he did not want to touch anything and pick up a scent on his skin. As soon as he walked into the church he went into reaction, and I had some Asian friends of mine pray for him.

Bruce had been told by his phone minister to go forward when they made a call for prayer that pertained to his situation. Once they began praying for people, two Chinese ladies came up to Bruce and urged him to come up to the altar. They were very short and he was very tall, but they were dragging him forward. Mahesh came up to him and asked him what was the matter with him. Bruce began explaining about MCS/EI. Mahesh interrupted and said that God can heal anything. He cast out spirits of infirmity and insanity, laid hands on him, and Bruce fell out under the power of the Holy Ghost.

When he became fully conscious of his surroundings, the Chinese ladies were praying for him in tongues, or maybe it was Chinese. There he was, lying on a rug, something no E.I. person would do. He was repeating, "Thank you God," and at that point he did not really know what had happened. He could not breathe in his respirator so he took it off, and when he did he could smell again, and he did not have a reaction. He went up to Mahesh to tell him what had happened when he, Mahesh, thrust a microphone at Bruce and urged him to share his testimony. All Bruce could say was, "Thank you God." The very next thing that happened was that he was on the stage getting his picture taken with the evangelist, who said that it is easier to get someone healed of AIDS in Africa than of a hangnail in America because of all the unbelief and doubt. Bruce was the only one healed that night.

The next day I insisted that Bruce get out, and that he go to church. I was concerned that he would fall back into old patterns after he returned home. We attended another large church service in San Francisco where the evangelist spoke again. At this service there was a deaf boy who got his hearing back, but it did not last. It was sad that the church did not know how to help him walk it out. If it had not been for the teaching and ministry at Pleasant Valley Church, I don't think Bruce would have kept his healing.

After the service I took Bruce to MacDonald's for a Big Mac. He was on his own after that, and he began to seriously walk out his deliverance. He began to walk around his neighborhood smelling car exhaust, smoke, paint, pesticide, roof tar, etc. He went to other fast food restaurants. He attended a small house church in his neighborhood.

One day I visited a park that was high on a cliff over looking the Pacific Ocean in San Francisco. It was very cold and windy, and I was afraid to get out of the car because of the wind. Pastor Henry had ministered to me from the first chapter of Joshua previously, and I sat in the car reading the Scripture, encouraging myself and building myself up in faith.

> **Every place that the sole of your foot shall tread upon, that have I given unto you, as I said unto Moses. From the wilderness and this Lebanon even unto the great river, the river Euphrates, all the land of the Hittites, and unto the great sea toward the going down of the sun, shall be your coast. There shall not any man be able to stand before thee all the days of thy life: as I was with Moses, so I will be with thee: I will not fail thee, nor forsake thee. Be strong and of a good courage. . . Joshua 1:3-6**

> **Have not I commanded thee? Be strong and of a good courage; be not afraid, neither be dismayed: for the LORD thy God is with thee whithersoever thou goest. Joshua 1:9**

After this I was able to get out of the car and walk around the park in the cold wind.

I have noticed that men seem to walk out of MCS/EI faster that most women. I think once they comprehend it is fear that is causing most of their reactions, they want no part of it. In defense of their masculinity they will rid themselves of fear. I remember one man who opened up his telephone book and used it for a pillow because he had been sensitive to the ink

166

in the print. But then I also know a woman who slept with an open can of paint under her bed because she was taking back her right to be around fresh paint. I do know that some people have been much braver than myself and more aggressive in facing their fears. One thing is for sure; you cannot turn your back on fear and avoid it. Walk-out involves facing every one of your fears. You can take a long time to do it, or you can get it done quickly. The choice is ours. Some fears I faced early, and others took much longer.

I acquired two small kittens when I was still allergic to cats. I took them on faith and was strongly motivated as I missed having a cat for a pet. When I was sick the only thing I could tolerate was goldfish. It is very hard to hug a goldfish. I had no problems with my kittens other than their climbing up my leg digging their claws in as if I were a tree. As they grew older, I grew up in the Lord.

During the summer of 1993, I went to Maui with my Christian friend. Anita was flying in from the East Coast and meeting us there for a celebration of our healing. I faced many challenges during this trip. First there was the long plane ride, and that went well. When we arrived I was confronted by the wind. I had forgotten how windy it was in Hawaii, and I still had fear about wind. Subsequently I was short of breath.

At that time Pastor Henry did not have the understanding that he does today of the role memories play in activating old symptoms. The wind was a stressor for me and set off the memory of past reactions to wind and the fear of past reactions. This was enough for me to go into reaction. I was in a fierce battle the rest of the day.

On Sunday we attended a small Hawaiian Pentecostal church where they rolled up the canvas sides of the church so the island breezes could blow through. Again I was battling tightness in my chest and problems breathing. After the service my friend spoke to the pastor on my behalf and asked him to pray for me. He asked a few people to join him, and while he was praying for me one lady began to weep. I did not understand why she was crying; I thought it strange that she should cry over me when she did not even know me. But after their prayer the symptoms left and did not return.

Anita arrived a couple of days later, and we did more walk-out. We decided to go parasailing to further confront our fears. I was making a strong statement that I had been healed of symptoms brought on by the wind. The plastic chair that we went up in had no seat belt nor did it have a bar across to hold on to like they have on a ferris wheel. We were up there in the sky just as if we were sitting in our living room. I have pictures of before we went up in the air with the parachute and after we landed, and we looked a whole lot happier after we came down! That day they were burning the sugar cane on the island, and there was a lot of smoke in the air. So not only were we exposed to the wind but also the smoke. More victory!

One day we drove to Hana, which is at the far end of the island. The road is rather primitive with lots of bumps and ruts. Since I had a chronic back condition, I had fear of going over that road, but I did fine with no back pain. I also took a picture of that bumpy road to be able to say I survived driving for miles on this road.

I had one lingering symptom that had not budged since I initially went to Pleasant Valley Church almost a year before. That was the vibration I had during my sleep. I would wake up every morning with my nervous system vibrating. This was the symptom that no doctor had been able to explain to me. It was during this trip to Hawaii that Anita did some pretty fierce praying on my behalf, and the symptom finally dissipated. The root was fear and stress. I did not know why some fear symptoms left easily, and others like this one remained, but it finally did leave after doing some spiritual warfare.

During this trip I also faced barbeque smoke and cigarette smoke coming from the terrace right next door to us. I went swimming every day in a chlorinated pool. We went to restaurants, and we visited one of the palatial hotels that had various objects from the occult as their décor. I could walk amongst these pagan artifacts without any ill effects as long as I had no fear of evil.

My walkout continued over the next year. Bruce and I shared our testimony in several churches in the San Francisco bay area. We taught on the occult at Shiloh Bible College in Oakland. Later I gave a teaching there by myself and had an interesting experience. I had some concern about being able to speak and project my voice over a large room of people for two continuous hours. When I arrived at the Bible college there was a big sign on the door that said: The youth are doing a play tonight, and they are using chemical fog. Do not enter if you have asthma or respiratory problems. I was taken aback. I had never seen a sign like this on the door before, and I was teaching in a classroom just off of the auditorium. I stopped for a minute and entertained some anxiety. I asked myself, "Do I have asthma?" Then the thought came, "No, you don't. You have been healed." I entered the school, taught my class and was unaware of anything going on in the adjacent auditorium.

Since my initial healing I have driven across the U.S. two times. On one of those trips I stopped to visit old friends, some of whom had E.I. and some did not. My first stop was in Texas to visit a college friend. I had no trouble staying in her house that smelled of mothballs. Perhaps others would not have noticed it, but at my stage of walk-out it smelled pretty strong. I had been taught, "It is just a smell. It won't harm you." In any case I did fine in her house.

In New Mexico we stopped to see some old friends with MCS/EI who had moved from the Bay area to New Mexico for the good, clean air. I was visiting someone who lived on the top of a hill secluded from other people, and while we were sitting outside in this pristine environment, I shared my testimony of healing. She had music on in the house, and I could hear in the background this sitar music and words that were saying guru this and guru that. My head started to swim; I was getting dizzy and having problems putting two thoughts together. I knew she would not understand if I told her that the Indian music was making me sick, so I just made a request that she turn it off. She looked at me a little strangely, but she turned it off. I was all right after that.

We visited another friend in New Mexico whose house was stripped down, no rugs or curtains, very little furniture, air filters in every room, etc. It was an E.I. "safe haven" without environmental toxins. I also reacted in this environment. I was puzzled. I could go into normal homes without any problem, but when I visited these friends in their safe environments, I had problems.

The last person we stopped to visit also had environmental illness, and her house was rather bare. She too had removed all the rugs, curtains etc. However, this woman was a strong Christian, and she had been having phone ministry with Pleasant Valley Church. I was fine in her house!

I learned a lot from these experiences. What made me sick was the spiritual dynamics of a home, not what cleaning supplies, rugs, furnishings, etc. were there. Pastor Henry was correct when he said that it is internal chemistry that makes an E.I. person ill, not the chemistry in the environment.

I have been to Europe twice and have traveled much in the United States. For many years I traveled back and forth between Pleasant Valley Church and California. At age fifty-seven I officially moved to Thomaston, Georgia, to serve the Lord through Be In Health™ Global, a ministry of Pleasant Valley Church.

I began teaching on occultism at the For My Life™ and For Their Life™ conferences and continue to do so today. I have had such a desire in my heart to see people set free from occultism, for them to be able to discern what is of God and what is not. For many years I served in phone ministry giving back what I had received. It is such an awesome privilege to serve the Lord on this level, helping His people to be delivered and to be healed. Father God answered my prayer when I cried out to Him in my sickness and told Him I wanted to make a difference in others' lives.

As part of my walk-out I have returned to some of my creative hobbies, and the Lord has been very good to me in this area: sewing, needlework, playing a keyboard and photography. My photos have been juried into several photography exhibits, and I have even won some awards. What is so amazing is that the only photography class I have taken in my life was to learn how to use a digital camera. The Lord gave me an eye for seeing the beauty of His creation. My friend Ellen and I exhibited our photography together at the local arts council. Each day is exciting with many activities to choose from. The Lord has truly restored my life.

One of the most difficult things I have had to face since I was healed was the death of my Mother in the year 2000. But even in that the Lord has been very good to me. He kept my mother alive until a time when I was well enough to be able to go to her and help her.

I had missed her eightieth birthday party because I was housebound at the time, so when she turned ninety my aunt and I threw her a birthday party. I invited all the old people from our neighborhood because my mother still lived in the house that my parents bought when I was three months old. Leading up to the party my mother was negative and critical of my decisions regarding the party. I wanted her to have her hair done a few days early so she would look nice for the party. She refused and would not alter her schedule.

In spite of our differences, the party was a huge success, with many old friends attending whom we had not seen in years. Everyone said it was a great party. Hardly any food was eaten because everyone was too busy talking with old friends. I had asked the guests to submit a written account of what they remembered about my mother and many of them did. We had a wonderful time reminiscing.

My mother lived another two years and it was in that last year of life that I had a revelation about her. I realized that she had a critical spirit. It did not matter what I did, she would be critical of it. She was critical of small things, how I drove the car, how big my purse was, how I styled my hair, and so forth. What a revelation! I had spent my whole life trying to win her approval and love, but I could not because she always disapproved. And it wasn't because of me; it was a spirit. The sad part was how so much of my life was in reaction to her. I wanted her love, and what I did not realize was that she loved me all along. She just happened to have a critical spirit.

My mother developed cancer in her ninety-second year of life. I praise God that He sustained her life long enough so that I would be healed and able to help her at the end when she needed me. She had a strong desire never to be a burden and never to have to go to a nursing home. She was driving her car up to the last month of her life. It made no difference that the neighbors were calling me long distance and telling me that they didn't think my mother should be driving. Driving was her independence, and she was not going to give it up, not if she had any say in the matter.

She was hospitalized during the last two weeks of her life. She had accepted the Lord about a year earlier, and when I questioned her, she made it clear that she had invited Him into her heart MORE THAN ONCE. Okay, it was settled. She was alert until she died, and she was working her favorite puzzles from the newspaper the night before she died. She could not see the letters, and I wrote them very large for her. She still got the correct answers to the word jumble, something I have never been good at doing.

The last day she declined very fast. The doctor told me that her organs were failing and she had a few days to live. I told her to talk to God about it, and I left the room to call her brother and sister. When I returned a short time later she was drawing her last breath. The Lord must have heard her prayer and did not let her suffer.

It was in the planning of her funeral and in talking with friends and neighbors that I got such a picture of my mother's love for me. Apparently she talked to them about me and how proud she was of me. She never told me this to my face, but I could hear it in the stories they told.

Selling my family home was one of the more emotionally difficult things I have had to do in my life.

173

Sixty years of our lives were stored there. It took quite a bit of work to get the house ready to put it up for sale. I could have sold the house as is, but I wanted it to look good, so I arranged for some painting, new linoleum, etc. I was pleased with the job I had done, and I left to come back to Georgia the day the house went on the market. On the flight back I had a conversation with God, and I told Him that I wanted to find a used house that had lovingly been cared for and that was very clean for a price I could afford.

I found such a house in a perfect location with a beautiful view out in the country. The floor plan was just what I was looking for. It was immaculately clean. Only one problem existed – I had cerebral reactions every time I entered the house. This was a total shock to me because it had been many years since I had had a cerebral reaction. I was not restricted by anything in my environment, so what was happening? I had friends who had a good sense of smell check it out, and they could detect nothing. I remember telling Pastor Donna Wright about finding this house and the problem I was having. She looked me straight in the eyes and said, "It sounds like the perfect house for you, Marcia." I got it! It was the perfect house; the only thing keeping me from it was a spirit of fear.

So I bought the house. The wonderful thing that God did was to find me a house for exactly what I could afford. When all was said and done there was a one dollar difference between the sale of my mother's property and this house. I told this story in church, and afterward a friend came up to give me a dollar. I said, "No, I had one dollar too much."

But I continued to have severe problems every time I came into the house to move small items in. One night several of us went over and walked through the empty rooms praying, claiming the house for me and the Lord, and commanding evil spirits to leave. I continued to feel so dizzy every time I entered the house. Finally the day arrived when I was scheduled to move in. Several friends from the church had volunteered to help me move. I was more than a little concerned, because so far these symptoms had not abated. What was I going to do if I continued to react? I had set myself on a course, and I was moving ahead with my life.

The day I moved in the reactions stopped, never to return again. So what was that? I can only believe that a spirit of fear was trying to snare me into believing that I couldn't have this house, and if I had believed him I never would have had the blessing God wanted me to have.

I could continue with walk-out stories because life is a walk-out, if not from an illness, then walk-out from the spiritual roots that are in our families and our own lives. In the course of living we are presented with opportunities to choose God's ways or the ways of the Devil. Every experience is an open door to either God or the Devil, to life or to death. What will you chose?

> **See, I have set before thee this day life and good, death and evil; In that I command thee this day to love the LORD thy God, to walk in his ways, and to keep his commandments, and his statutes and his judgments, that thou mayest live and multiply: and the LORD thy God shall bless thee in the land whither thou goest to possess it. Deuteronomy 30:15-16**

This seems like a natural place to close these chapters of my life. It has been my purpose in sharing my story to encourage others who are ill, disabled, broken hearted, lost in the occult, into all kinds of sin. God loves you. He is no respecter of persons, and what He did for me, He will do for you. No one's circumstances are too much for Him to handle. He is in the business of transforming lives. Come to Him; invite Jesus to be Lord over your life; let Him into your heart. You too may be healed, and He will also put a new song into your heart.

I waited patiently for the LORD; and he inclined unto me, and heard my cry. He brought me up also out of an horrible pit, out of the miry clay, and set my foot upon a rock, and established my goings. And he hath put a new song in my mouth, even praise unto our God; many shall see it, and fear, and shall trust in the LORD.
Psalm 40:1-3

GLORY TO GOD!

Appendix A (Scripture)

Psalm 51

[1] Have mercy upon me, O God, according to thy lovingkindness: according unto the multitude of thy tender mercies blot out my transgressions.

[2] Wash me throughly from mine iniquity, and cleanse me from my sin.

[3] For I acknowledge my transgressions: and my sin is ever before me.

[4] Against thee, thee only, have I sinned, and done this evil in thy sight: that thou mightest be justified when thou speakest, and be clear when thou judgest.

[5] Behold, I was shapen in iniquity; and in sin did my mother conceive me.

[6] Behold, thou desirest truth in the inward parts: and in the hidden part thou shalt make me to know wisdom.

[7] Purge me with hyssop, and I shall be clean: wash me, and I shall be whiter than snow.

[8] Make me to hear joy and gladness; that the bones which thou hast broken may rejoice.

[9] Hide thy face from my sins, and blot out all mine iniquities.

[10] Create in me a clean heart, O God; and renew a right spirit within me.

[11] Cast me not away from thy presence; and take not thy holy spirit from me.

[12] Restore unto me the joy of thy salvation; and uphold me with thy free spirit.

[13] Then will I teach transgressors thy ways; and sinners shall be converted unto thee.

¹⁴ Deliver me from bloodguiltiness, O God, thou God of my salvation: and my tongue shall sing aloud of thy righteousness.

¹⁵ O Lord, open thou my lips; and my mouth shall shew forth thy praise.

¹⁶ For thou desirest not sacrifice; else would I give it: thou delightest not in burnt offering.

¹⁷ The sacrifices of God are a broken spirit: a broken and a contrite heart, O God, thou wilt not despise.

¹⁸ Do good in thy good pleasure unto Zion: build thou the walls of Jerusalem.

Psalm 91

¹ He that dwelleth in the secret place of the most High shall abide under the shadow of the Almighty.

² I will say of the LORD, He is my refuge and my fortress: my God; in him will I trust.

³ Surely he shall deliver thee from the snare of the fowler, and from the noisome pestilence.

⁴ He shall cover thee with his feathers, and under his wings shalt thou trust: his truth shall be thy shield and buckler.

⁵ Thou shalt not be afraid for the terror by night; nor for the arrow that flieth by day;

⁶ Nor for the pestilence that walketh in darkness; nor for the destruction that wasteth at noonday.

⁷ A thousand shall fall at thy side, and ten thousand at thy right hand; but it shall not come nigh thee.

⁸ Only with thine eyes shalt thou behold and see the reward of the wicked.

⁹ Because thou hast made the LORD, which is my refuge, even the most High, thy habitation;

¹⁰ There shall no evil befall thee, neither shall any plague come nigh thy dwelling.

¹¹ For he shall give his angels charge over thee, to keep thee in all thy ways.

¹² They shall bear thee up in their hands, lest thou dash thy foot against a stone.

¹³ Thou shalt tread upon the lion and adder: the young lion and the dragon shalt thou trample under feet.

¹⁴ Because he hath set his love upon me, therefore will I deliver him: I will set him on high, because he hath known my name.

¹⁵ He shall call upon me, and I will answer him: I will be with him in trouble; I will deliver him, and honour him.

¹⁶ With long life will I satisfy him, and shew him my salvation.

Psalm 103

¹ Bless the LORD, O my soul: and all that is within me, bless his holy name.

² Bless the LORD, O my soul, and forget not all his benefits:

³ Who forgiveth all thine iniquities; who healeth all thy diseases;

⁴ Who redeemeth thy life from destruction; who crowneth thee with lovingkindness and tender mercies;

⁵ Who satisfieth thy mouth with good things; so that thy youth is renewed like the eagle's.

⁶ The LORD executeth righteousness and judgment for all that are oppressed.

⁷ He made known his ways unto Moses, his acts unto the children of Israel.

⁸ The LORD is merciful and gracious, slow to anger, and plenteous in mercy.

⁹ He will not always chide: neither will he keep his anger for ever.

¹⁰ He hath not dealt with us after our sins; nor rewarded us according to our iniquities.

¹¹ For as the heaven is high above the earth, so great is his mercy toward them that fear him.

¹² As far as the east is from the west, so far hath he removed our transgressions from us.

¹³ Like as a father pitieth his children, so the LORD pitieth them that fear him.

¹⁴ For he knoweth our frame; he remembereth that we are dust.

¹⁵ As for man, his days are as grass: as a flower of the field, so he flourisheth.

¹⁶ For the wind passeth over it, and it is gone; and the place thereof shall know it no more.

¹⁷ But the mercy of the LORD is from everlasting to everlasting upon them that fear him, and his righteousness unto children's children;

¹⁸ To such as keep his covenant, and to those that remember his commandments to do them.

¹⁹ The LORD hath prepared his throne in the heavens; and his kingdom ruleth over all.

²⁰ Bless the LORD, ye his angels, that excel in strength, that do his commandments, hearkening unto the voice of his word.

²¹ Bless ye the LORD, all ye his hosts; ye ministers of his, that do his pleasure.

²² Bless the LORD, all his works in all places of his dominion: bless the LORD, O my soul.

Psalm 104

¹ Bless the LORD, O my soul. O LORD my God, thou art very great; thou art clothed with honour and majesty.

² Who coverest thyself with light as with a garment: who stretchest out the heavens like a curtain:

³ Who layeth the beams of his chambers in the waters: who maketh the clouds his chariot: who walketh upon the wings of the wind:

⁴ Who maketh his angels spirits; his ministers a flaming fire:

⁵ Who laid the foundations of the earth, that it should not be removed for ever.

⁶ Thou coveredst it with the deep as with a garment: the waters stood above the mountains.

⁷ At thy rebuke they fled; at the voice of thy thunder they hasted away.

⁸ They go up by the mountains; they go down by the valleys unto the place which thou hast founded for them.

⁹ Thou hast set a bound that they may not pass over; that they turn not again to cover the earth.

¹⁰ He sendeth the springs into the valleys, which run among the hills.

¹¹ They give drink to every beast of the field: the wild asses quench their thirst.

¹² By them shall the fowls of the heaven have their habitation, which sing among the branches.

¹³ He watereth the hills from his chambers: the earth is satisfied with the fruit of thy works.

¹⁴ He causeth the grass to grow for the cattle, and herb for the service of man: that he may bring forth food out of the earth;

¹⁵ And wine that maketh glad the heart of man, and oil to make his face to shine, and bread which strengtheneth man's heart.

¹⁶ The trees of the LORD are full of sap; the cedars of Lebanon, which he hath planted;

¹⁷ Where the birds make their nests: as for the stork, the fir trees are her house.

¹⁸ The high hills are a refuge for the wild goats; and the rocks for the conies.

¹⁹ He appointed the moon for seasons: the sun knoweth his going down.

²⁰ Thou makest darkness, and it is night: wherein all the beasts of the forest do creep forth.

²¹ The young lions roar after their prey, and seek their meat from God.

²² The sun ariseth, they gather themselves together, and lay them down in their dens.

²³ Man goeth forth unto his work and to his labour until the evening.

²⁴ O LORD, how manifold are thy works! in wisdom hast thou made them all: the earth is full of thy riches.

²⁵ So is this great and wide sea, wherein are things creeping innumerable, both small and great beasts.

²⁶ There go the ships: there is that leviathan, whom thou hast made to play therein.

²⁷ These wait all upon thee; that thou mayest give them their meat in due season.

²⁸ That thou givest them they gather: thou openest thine hand, they are filled with good.

²⁹ Thou hidest thy face, they are troubled: thou takest away their breath, they die, and return to their dust.

³⁰ Thou sendest forth thy spirit, they are created: and thou renewest the face of the earth.

³¹ The glory of the LORD shall endure for ever: the LORD shall rejoice in his works.

³² He looketh on the earth, and it trembleth: he toucheth the hills, and they smoke.

³³ I will sing unto the LORD as long as I live: I will sing praise to my God while I have my being.

³⁴ My meditation of him shall be sweet: I will be glad in the LORD.

³⁵ Let the sinners be consumed out of the earth, and let the wicked be no more. Bless thou the LORD, O my soul. Praise ye the LORD.

Psalm 139

[1] O LORD, thou hast searched me, and known me.

[2] Thou knowest my downsitting and mine uprising, thou understandest my thought afar off.

[3] Thou compassest my path and my lying down, and art acquainted with all my ways.

[4] For there is not a word in my tongue, but, lo, O LORD, thou knowest it altogether.

[5] Thou hast beset me behind and before, and laid thine hand upon me.

[6] Such knowledge is too wonderful for me; it is high, I cannot attain unto it.

[7] Whither shall I go from thy spirit? or whither shall I flee from thy presence?

[8] If I ascend up into heaven, thou art there: if I make my bed in hell, behold, thou art there.

[9] If I take the wings of the morning, and dwell in the uttermost parts of the sea;

[10] Even there shall thy hand lead me, and thy right hand shall hold me.

[11] If I say, Surely the darkness shall cover me; even the night shall be light about me.

[12] Yea, the darkness hideth not from thee; but the night shineth as the day: the darkness and the light are both alike to thee.

[13] For thou hast possessed my reins: thou hast covered me in my mother's womb.

[14] I will praise thee; for I am fearfully and wonderfully made: marvellous are thy works; and that my soul knoweth right well.

[15] My substance was not hid from thee, when I was made in secret, and curiously wrought in the lowest parts of the earth.

[16] Thine eyes did see my substance, yet being unperfect; and in thy book all my members were written, which

in continuance were fashioned, when as yet there was none of them.

¹⁷ How precious also are thy thoughts unto me, O God! how great is the sum of them!

¹⁸ If I should count them, they are more in number than the sand: when I awake, I am still with thee.

¹⁹ Surely thou wilt slay the wicked, O God: depart from me therefore, ye bloody men.

²⁰ For they speak against thee wickedly, and thine enemies take thy name in vain.

²¹ Do not I hate them, O LORD, that hate thee? and am not I grieved with those that rise up against thee?

²² I hate them with perfect hatred: I count them mine enemies.

²³ Search me, O God, and know my heart: try me, and know my thoughts:

²⁴ And see if there be any wicked way in me, and lead me in the way everlasting.

Appendix B (Doctor's Letter)

JEFFRY L. ANDERSON, M.D.
45 San Clemente Dr., Suite B-100, B-110
Corte Madera, CA 94925
(415) 927-7140

September 29, 1989

Re: Marcia Fisher

To Whom It May Concern:

Ms. Marcia Fisher has been under my care since 1987 for a severe and chronic immune system disorder characterized by chronic fatigue immunodeficiency syndrome, autoimmune endocrinopathy, and severe exquisite allergic and hypersensitivity reactions to a diffuse number of environmental factors, possibly associated with bioaccumulation of chemical solvents from occupational exposures in the past. She has extensive allergic and hypersensitivity reactions to environmental molds and mildews, severe reactions to a diverse number of chemical agents commonly found in most environments including perfumes and other scented products, tobacco smoke, auto and diesel exhaust, natural gas as well as propane and butane, most aliphatic and aromatic as well as chlorinated solvents, commonly used pesticides, newsprint, formaldehyde, and isocyanates related to decorative and constructive materials, etc. Some of her reactions can produce disabling exhaustion, organic brain dysfunction, respiratory symptoms including marked reactive airway disease-extrinsic asthma, severe musculoskeletal and neuritic pain, and vertiginous dizziness. Some manifestations are severe enough to be life threatening if exposure is prolonged or concentrated.

She requires very strict and impeccable environmental control, particularly in her indoor environment which can be her only safe haven. She will require, therefore, a one bedroom apartment so that she can utilize the bedroom as her one safe room to be isolated from the rest of the apartment. Cooking fumes, dust, mold spores, outdoor air contaminants, etc. which can enter the general apartment area be minimized in a small bedroom utilizing extensive air quality modification with state-of-the-art air filtration and purification systems, dehumidifying compounds such as silica crystals, and other procedures. It would be impossible to control the air quality in a whole apartment which has open communication between all areas including bathroom, kitchen, outdoor air sources, etc.

If you have any further questions, please do not hesitate to contact me.[37]

---

[37] This is an edited copy of the original letter.

Appendix C (Victory List)

The following is a list of things I had to take back from the enemy. Every hypersensitivity reaction and allergic response represented a fear in my life. I avoided so many things that I eventually became housebound, isolated from people and life. In taking back my land I had to face every fear and walk through the experience. Just as God told Joshua to defeat all his enemies, I had to do the same. God gave Joshua the land, but he had to go in to possess it. You cannot do this alone under your own strength, but you can do it with the Lord.

Cigarette smoke – in the airport, the bowling alley, restaurants and riding in a car with people who had smoke on their clothes

Perfume – in church, hugging people who wore perfume, living in the same house with those who wore perfume, riding in a car with someone wearing perfume

New clothes – wearing a hat right out of the store, wearing new clothes after only one washing, wearing the fabric or color I wanted

Laundromats with gas dryers, using them to wash and dry my clothes

Sleeping on freshly washed sheets

Grocery store - detergent aisle

Riding in a car without an air filter

Drying clothes on the line outside

Fresh air, wind – being able to go outside without a mask or respirator

Car exhaust – living on a busy street

Air conditioning

Visited a newly painted house

Food – beef, pork, dairy products, sugar, raw vegetables, wheat, fast foods, sodas, candy

Tap water

Clorox, Lysol spray, Pine-Sol

Read my new Bible after airing only one month

Went to a brand new department store soon after it opened

Went to Home Depot and the Dollar Store (smelly places)

Riding in the car with the window down — riding in a car with the air conditioner bringing in outside air

Commercial shampoo

Chewing gum

Indiana trip — airplane ride without mask or oxygen, slept on bedding washed in Clorox, stayed in a house with residual cigarette smoke, used towels dried in Bounce, rode in a brand new minivan, attended a concert in a large auditorium filled with people, went to a basketball game.

Antibiotics — a pill with blue dye

Campfire smoke

The mall by myself for three hours trying on clothes

An evening by the fireplace with candles burning

Long airplane rides – airplane food

Coffee and soft drinks

Stayed in a motel

Raid

New rugs

Cats and dogs

Spring pollens and everyday mold

A More Excellent Way
Be in Health™
Henry W Wright

Out of Many Waters
Anita Hill
with
Kim Pearson Wiese